Making Shots—A Rifle Hunter's Guide

Hunting Wisdom Library™

MINNETONKA, MINNESOTA

About the Author

Bryce M. Towsley is an award-winning writer and photographer whose work covers a wide diversity of subjects—but none more than the field of big game hunting and the rifles used for that sport.

In the past two decades Towsley has published hundreds of articles and thousands of photos in most of the major outdoor magazines. This is his second hunting-related book.

Towsley is a dedicated gun buff and has been reloading since he was 11 years old. He is an avid hunter with more than 33 years of experience, taking his first whitetail in Vermont in 1966 at the age of 11. Since then, he has hunted extensively throughout North America for a wide variety of game.

Towsley lives in Vermont with his wife, Robin, and children Erin and Nathan.

MAKING SHOTS—A RIFLE HUNTER'S GUIDE

Mike Vail
Vice President, Product and Business Development

Tom Carpenter
Director of Book and New Media Development

Dan Kennedy
Book Production Manager, Photo Editor

Heather Koshiol
Book Development Coordinator

Dave Schelitzche
Book Design and Production

Phil Aarrestad
Commissioned Photography

PHOTO CREDITS

All photos by Bryce Towsley except: 2, John Kascenska; 5, Jeff Boehler; cover onlay, 30, 32, 33, 60, 74, 93, 155, Phil Aarestad; 39 (2), 94, 159 (2), Tom Carpenter; 43, Rob Rundquist; 51, 166, 172, 173, Lee Kline; 53, Bill Marchel; 95, Mark Kayser; 141, Dan Kennedy; 148, Denver Bryan; 168, 169, 170, 171, Lance Kreuger.

1 2 3 4 5 6 7 8 / 02 01 00 99

ISBN 1-58159-095-4

North American Hunting Club
12301 Whitewater Drive
Minnetonka, Minnesota 55343

Table of Contents

Foreword

A hunter carries two kinds of tools. The first kind resides in your head—your understanding of the game, your familiarity with the land, and of course the strategies and even the attitude you take to the hunt.

Then consider the items you carry, wear and use—warm and quiet clothes, binoculars, good boots, a sharp knife, calls or rattling antlers or grunt tubes or decoys ... if you pack like me, this list could continue for awhile.

But of all these ideas, all this *stuff*, there is only one thing you absolutely and positively cannot do without: something to shoot with. Take away my hat. Make it foggy so my binoculars are worthless. Put me in a pair of tennis shoes. Steal my good blade and leave me with only my pocket knife. But don't take away my rifle!

In the end, all the planning you do, the gear you buy, the preparations you make, the daydreams you live by ... it all comes down to your rifle and a shot. That's why we created this book, *Making Shots*, and then dubbed it *A Rifle Hunter's Guide*.

Of course, we found the best in the business—Bryce Towsley—to bring it all together for you. This guy is a straight shooter—with a rifle in his hands most certainly but more importantly for you, in the way he goes about teaching you how to be a better, more confident and more accurate shot in the field.

This isn't one of those dry, yawner gun books you see around. This is a hunting book for every hunter who uses a rifle. If you want to keep your rifles in top condition, shoot better all the time, make all your work pay off when that critical moment arrives ... this book is for you.

I love hunting, just being out there—most anywhere—with a rifle in my hands or slung over my shoulder. But I also like to get what I'm searching for, when the opportunity arises. *Making Shots* is going to take me there more often, and it will do that for you too.

Tom

Tom Carpenter
Editor
North American Hunting Club Books

INTRODUCTION

When I was a kid, my heroes were never baseball, basketball or football players. They weren't fire fighters, police officers or soldiers, and they certainly weren't politicians. My heroes were the guys who brought Africa, Alaska and the American West to my house each month and the guys who introduced me to the new guns and high-performance cartridges.

They inspired my imagination and fueled my desire to see the world with a gun in my hand. They sparked a love for guns and ignited a longing for adventure that continues to grow with each breath I take. My heroes brought me to places unknown in the boring confines of a stuffy schoolroom locked in a small town, and they showed me possibilities that didn't exist in my world. They inspired me and motivated me. My heroes were the gun and hunting writers of the 1950s, '60s and '70s.

Those who are caught up in this wonderful world of big game hunting and rifle shooting are the only kind of people I ever feel truly comfortable around. The hunters I understand best are the ones who think of rifles as both precision machines and as works of art … who think of each cartridge as a unique personality. They like to have guns, to hold them and admire the fine lines, to possess them and simply to look at them. They appreciate the intricate beauty in the subtle patterns of a fine walnut stock as well as the stark contrasts and the pragmatic design of a stainless steel, synthetic-stocked rifle. For them, as well as me, ballistics shrouded in mystery are only a challenge to be explored, and the marriage of machinery and physics that allows a rifle to operate is both science and art.

My fascination with rifles and cartridges has led me down some interesting paths. There are so many forks in the road leading to intriguing guns and cartridges that I expect the journey will continue for a long time still.

My beliefs about big game rifles and what works stem from years of personal observation coupled with interviews of hundreds of outfitters and thousands of hunters. Some are gun writers but most have simply been contacts made through nearly 20 years of writing about guns and hunting, and 15 years as a booking agent for big game hunting. My opinions all stem from a passionate need to know what works and what does not. To those of you who have called to talk hunting and endured the endless interrogation about the performance of your rifles, cartridges and bullets, thanks … you helped write this book.

Bryce M Townsley

Chapter 1

THE RIFLE

*S*hooters tend to be a conservative lot, and gun evolution has been anything but rapid.

Depending on the historical text you consult, it would appear that the Chinese had some sort of gunpowder as early as the 11th century. The Western world was introduced to gunpowder by Roger Bacon in 1248. The first handheld gun, or "Hand Gonne," emerged around 1350. Things remained more or less status quo for about 500 years, until the early 19th century saw the emergence of both rifling and percussion ignition, which started a mini-revolution in firearms development. (Actually, rifling was known as early as 1540, but technical difficulties kept it from common use until the 19th century.)

This century's technology boom has brought great performance advances in sporting firearms. Computers and their use in design and manufacturing have advanced the speed of the firearms revolution as well as the accuracy, reliability and power of today's rifles. But these changes are primarily in functional design; the looks and aesthetics of hunting rifles change more slowly. Certainly, a new bolt-action, stainless steel, synthetic-stock rifle looks a bit different from a Winchester 1873 lever action, but an old-time Texas cowboy would recognize it instantly as a rifle. Likewise, a modern-day hunter handling a rifle from the late 1800s certainly knows what he holds in his hands.

BOLT ACTIONS

oday the bolt action is the most popular, by far, of
sporting rifle designs. The question that many
uninformed ask is, why? Other than the single-
shot, it's the slowest action going. With pumps,
lever actions and semiautos all chambered for cartridges
up to and including the belted magnums, why are the bolt
actions so in demand?

Accuracy.

At least that's the primary answer to the question. The rest
of the equation includes reliability, strength, durability, versatility and dependability. But accuracy is the biggest reason.

ACCURATE

No other action is inherently as accurate as today's modern bolt-action rifle. Some single-shots come close, but in the
final analysis the bolt action is, on the average, simply a
more accurate design. Bolt guns also lend themselves better

Here's a Remington Model 700 Classic 7mm Rem. Mag. with Leupold Vari-X III 2.5-8 scope. This rifle and scope are among the best and most versatile available for hunting North American big game.

than any other rifle style to improving the already excellent out-of-the-box accuracy that most of today's guns exhibit.

The modern bolt action is receptive to simple accuracy improvements, such as bedding the action, floating the barrel or improving the trigger pull. One of the most important aspects of accurate rifle shooting is a good trigger pull, and as a rule, bolt actions usually have better triggers right from the factory than do other rifle action styles. By design, they also are much easier to replace with aftermarket triggers; or a gunsmith can improve the existing trigger.

If we take accuracy enhancement a step further and true the bolt with the barrel, lap the bolt lugs for even contact, minimize head space in the chamber and recrown the barrel, accuracy is further enhanced. Even these advanced improvements are simple compared to some of the gunsmithing work needed to improve other action types just enough to match accuracy levels that the best bolt actions exhibit right from the factory.

STRONG & RELIABLE

The bolt action is one of the strongest action designs. In repeating rifles, it's probably the strongest we have. If you are using modern high-pressure cartridges, then it's the best choice. For those approaching the SAAMI (Sporting Arms and Manufacturers Institute) pressure maximum and doing it in big cases, like the .300 Rem. Ultra Mag. or Wthby .30-378, it's the only sane choice in a repeating rifle.

The bolt action is reliable and not nearly as prone to jamming as some other action designs. If a problem develops for whatever reason, the bolt action has a lot more camming power to either close a balking action or to open one that's sticking. A bolt action will simply take more abuse and neglect and keep working than any other sporting repeating-action design.

It's not by accident that most professional hunters who guide for dangerous big game in Africa, Canada, Alaska or any other part of the world use bolt-action rifles.

These guides are not called upon to shoot until after trouble occurs, and they must have total reliability in their firearms.

These same reasons for selecting a bolt gun apply to all big-game hunters. Sure, you may never face a charging buffalo, but if you lose the whitetail buck of a lifetime because your rifle failed, it may seem just as bad. With the buffalo, you are merely dead; with the buck, you have the rest of your life to wish you were.

Bolt action rifles are simply the most reliable. You may never face a charging buffalo; but if you lose a whitetail buck like this one because your rifle failed, you'll feel even worse.

These traits of accuracy, dependability and durability are far more important to a big-game hunter than sheer firepower. The very fact that a bolt action is not capable of fast repeat shots (when compared to semiautos or pump actions) may also provide a psychological aspect that forces the hunter to shoot his or her best.

There are very few places in today's hunting world where a bolt action is not the best—or, at the very least, among the best—choice in a hunting rifle.

The bolt action rifle is the primary choice for today's Western big game hunter. And elsewhere in today's hunting world, a bolt action is usually among the best choices in a hunting rifle.

SINGLE-SHOTS

ingle-shot rifles are certainly not for everybody, and the rewards are something the masses will never experience or understand.

The disadvantages of single-shot rifles are quite obvious. They hold only one cartridge, and they are slow to reload and fire when compared to other modern sporting rifle designs.

SHORTER, EASY TO HANDLE

The advantages are more numerous and often more subtle. Perhaps the most obvious is the lack of a long receiver. This necessary component of other action designs can essentially be left off of a single-shot rifle. The result is that the overall length of the rifle is shortened by several inches.

Obviously, this creates a lighter gun, but in addition, it allows some flexibility in the barrel length. A standard-length barrel creates a gun that is much shorter in overall length than its repeating counterpart. These shorter rifles are handier to use in many hunting situations. The other end of the equation is that the barrel can be made longer while still maintaining a shorter rifle. The longer barrels will milk more performance out of most cartridges so that, in effect, you are adding a "supercharger" to your rifle.

FEELS GOOD

Those are tangible benefits for a single-shot rifle, but the more subjective benefits are no less real. Most shooters agree that the balance and "feel" of a single-shot rifle is like no

other. Many of the reasons why most serious wing shooters choose double shotguns and why many professional hunters of the golden era of African hunting selected double rifles center on the superb handling characteristics of these guns. The same qualities are seen in many single-shot rifles because the lack of a receiver moves the point of balance back on the gun. This balance, feel and handling of a single-shot has many hunters and shooters singing their praises. They are fast to use, point well and simply feel right in a hunter's hands.

The same might be said for the aesthetics of the single-shot. The lines and breeding for rifles like the Ruger Number One, the Dakota Number Ten and others are to many like those of a thoroughbred. Undeniably, these rifles are some of the most aesthetically pleasing and purest of form ever built.

SHOOTS WELL

Then there is the shooting factor. Most single-shots are fine shooting rifles, but on average they are not as accurate as their bolt-action counterparts. So why do so many hunters shoot them so well? The answer is found in the rifle design itself and in the mindset of the type of hunter who chooses to use them. The single-shot forces the hunter to recognize the importance of the first shot and to focus energy on making it count.

A good example of that is in an experiment I conducted a few years ago. I assembled a collection of five shooters of varying skill levels. Using a life-sized target of a white-tailed deer, they fired all rifle action designs in a test that measured both speed and accuracy. Two rifles of each action type were used for a series of three shot groups. The accuracy portion of the test used a scale on which nine points was perfect. The other action types—bolt, lever, pump and semiauto—were all within .75 of a point of each other for the final average. The best was the bolt action, with a score of 4.2; the lever action

Most shooters agree that the balance and "feel" of a single-shot rifle is like no other. A single-shot allows you to be fast on the target and point well. And it just feels right in your hands.

Single shots may be slower to load, but they have their assets too. This H&R rifle in .25-06 Remington is very affordable and amazingly accurate.

fared the poorest, with an average score of 3.45. As expected, the single-shots were the slowest and placed dead last on the speed phase of the test, but on the accuracy portion they scored an outstanding 6.45! This is a full 2.77 points better than the average for all the other action types and 2.25 points higher than the next best, the bolt action.

The single-shot's high score for accuracy wasn't because those rifles were built to be any more accurate. I have extensively tested all the guns, and the accuracy of the single-shots would fall somewhere slightly above the middle of the pack. The reason that the single-shots scored so well is that its shooters realized they couldn't do well on the timed portion of the test, so they concentrated on shooting well.

This same principle applies in the field. Most hunters would agree that when hunting with a single-shot rifle, they simply shoot better.

Single-shots are our oldest rifle design, but there is little danger that they will ever become obsolete. They simply have too much to offer for that to happen.

One shot is enough if you place it right. An H&R single shot rifle was more than adequate to take this tough feral hog.

LEVER ACTIONS

o you remember your first deer? Of course you do; every hunter does, including me. It was 1966, early morning on a school day. Dad and I were out for a quick hunt that ended in the best possible way for a hunting-crazy 11-year-old boy.

I can recall every detail, especially the gun I was using. It was, of course, a lever action. Just about every deer hunter I knew used one then. Dad had a Winchester Model 55 in .30-30 Win., Gramp used a Model 1886 in .45-70 Gov. and Uncle Butch had a Marlin Model 93 in .38-55. Mine was a Model 1892 Winchester in .38-40 that was loaned to me by my grandfather. It had been cut down to "kid" size by an unknown butcher, presumably with a dull chainsaw.

The gun was so badly worn out that it functioned without jamming only occasionally and probably wouldn't shoot a "minute of washtub" group at any distance. The caliber itself was undistinguished as a game killer. According to legend, its only redeeming quality was that it "had a bullet that made a big hole that lots of blood could run out of." To me, it was the finest deer rifle on earth.

The 1895 Marlin is responsible for the restored interest in the .45-70. Deep woods whitetail hunters love this rifle for its fast handling, while hunters all over North America are discovering that with proper loads, the .45-70 will take any game that walks the continent.

OLD STANDBY, STILL GREAT

Not surprisingly, many of the "best rifles made today" are still lever actions. America's first successful repeating rifle design is alive and well, and I continue to hunt with lever-action rifles each year. Not only for nostalgia, but because I believe that they are often the best rifle for the job. It may be an old design, but it remains an undisputed fact that a lever action is often one of the best choices a deer hunter can make.

OF BULLETS & CALIBERS

The downside for most lever actions is that pointed bullets cannot be used in the common tube-style magazines because the nose of the bullet rests on the primer of the cartridge ahead of it in the magazine. These cartridges are under pressure from the magazine spring, and the sharp impact from the recoil of firing can conceivably cause a pointed bullet to impact the primer of the cartridge in front of it hard enough to fire. As a result, any gun with a tube magazine must use only flat- or round-nosed bullets.

Flat- and round-nosed bullets are thought to be ballistically inferior to the pointed bullets that are in vogue with today's hunters, and on first glance they are. However, the other limitation of most lever actions is that the guns themselves are not particularly strong. That's not to say they are dangerous; they are not, but when compared to the strength of other action styles, such as a bolt action, the traditional lever-action design, like those used by Winchester and Marlin, is relatively weak and "springy." As a result, these guns are usually chambered for cartridges that operate under lower pressures than do many modern cartridges. These tend to be "short-range" cartridges designed for use

When November brings the first snow there is little on the mind of a whitetail hunter in the North or Northeast except the cold, spruce-scented air of the deep woods. This Winchester Model 94 in .30-30 Winchester has long been a favorite for these deer hunters.

You will find most lever-action rifles in the whitetail woods, but with cartridges such as the .444 Marlin or .45-70 Government, lever actions can handle any game in North America.

in the woods, and so blunt bullets are not the ballistic burden they would first appear to be. Don't sell them short, though; cartridges such as the .444 Marlin or .45-70 Gov., particularly when they are handloaded, can handle any game in North America.

While the Marlin, Winchester and most imported lever actions feature tubular magazines that require flat-point bullets, the Savage Model 99 introduced the lever action to modern calibers, such as the .308 Win. and .243 Win. It features a stronger action and a box magazine, so along with the higher pressures, pointed bullets are not a problem. The Browning BLR takes it a step further, with chambering options that include belted magnums.

Today's lever actions can cover everything from short-range, big-bullet thumpers to the barrel-stretching, long-range capabilities of a modern belted magnum; in other words, they provide something for everyone. Isn't it time you tried hunting with America's sweetheart rifle, the lever action?

SEMIAUTOS

A semiauto rifle fires once each time the trigger is pulled. Rather than requiring the shooter to work the action to chamber the next cartridge, it cycles the action using power supplied from bleeding off a little gas from the barrel.

Semiauto rifles can be great hunting firearms. Their biggest asset is that they are fast on the follow-up. Any good hunter strives to make the first shot count, but an experienced hunter knows the real world is sometimes a lot different. A fast second or third shot can often be crucial.

Unfortunately, these attributes attract a lot of hunters for the same reasons. They see firepower more than skill as the answer to hitting game.

Bucks that respond to antler rattling often come in pumped up and ready to rumble. When the action is fast many hunters prefer a semiauto rifle.

"RAMBO" & HIS SEMIAUTO

I remember back in the late 1980s one hunter whom I had booked to hunt Alberta whitetails the same week that I was in camp. He ignored my advice and that of the outfitter to bring one of his many bolt actions and showed up with an H&K semiauto in .30-06. This may have been acceptable because it was an accurate rifle in a flat-shooting cartridge. But the mind-set of the hunter was demonstrated the next day as we checked the sights on our rifles.

We were shooting at a couple of targets tacked to a 4- by 8-foot sheet of plywood placed 200 yards distant. All the other hunters, myself included, were shooting bolt-action rifles. Most were zeroed fine, but a few needed a little tweaking. Finally, "Mr. Automatic" stepped up to the shooting bench. Ten shots later, he had still not even hit the plywood. He refused to let any of us try the gun, and as his embarrassment mounted he suddenly announced, "This is how I do it!"

He stood up, pulled a high-capacity magazine from his pocket and proceeded to toss 15 or 20 rounds at the target as fast as he could pull the trigger. When we checked, a couple had actually hit the plywood, and he proudly stated, "Nothing could get out of that alive. Let's go hunting and I'll show you guys how it's done!"

In the area we were hunting, there was at least one world-class buck. The outfitter had watched him with a spotting scope enough that fall to know that he would score high in the record books. One hunter had him only 200 yards away the day after he had punched his ticket on a lesser buck, and he had a hard time even talking for hours. The deer was that good!

By now you may have guessed that the only one to get a shot at that buck was "Rambo," and he of course missed. Somehow—and I am still not clear on this—as the booking agent, it was all my fault.

ONLY IN THE RIGHT HANDS

This guy is only one of the far too many I have encountered in camps all over the country who mistake firepower for skill. They won't practice, or if they do, they blast away rapid-fire and build no shooting skills. With this "spray and pray" mentality, they think the answer to hitting game is to put a lot of lead in the air and hope something runs into it. It's these guys who always seem to be the reason we are out at midnight trying to follow skimpy blood trails with dying flashlights. They are exactly the reason that semiautos have a tarnished reputation in the hunting fields and with most guides.

It's not the guns—it's the hunters who use them. In competent and skilled hands (which are rare indeed), a semiauto can be an outstanding hunting rifle.

One often-ignored benefit of a semiauto hunting rifle is that no noise is necessary to prepare for the next shot. The action cycles so fast that the noise from the report and the action appear to be one and the same. Sometimes, when a game animal is missed with the first shot, it will freeze, confused about where the danger lies. The sound of an action being worked in any other type of rifle answers that question for them.

The semiauto hunting rifle field is not crowded, and fear of government regulation keeps it from growing. But those that are out there can be outstanding hunting guns, if they are used by the right hunters.

In competent and skilled hands, a semiauto can be an outstanding hunting rifle. This Texas buck fell to the author's first shot, but if another had been needed it was there and ready to go.

PUMP ACTIONS

Pump action guns have been around almost as long as self-contained cartridges have existed. While it is an immensely popular action style in shotguns, it has at best enjoyed a tepid following with rifle shooters. But the hunters who use them are extremely loyal and hunt with the unquestioned confidence that the pump action rifle they hold is the very best tool available for the job they have planned.

Most of those hunters are northeastern deer hunters, but I have seen pump rifles in such diverse places as New Brunswick, Texas, Wyoming, Alabama, and the Canadian arctic. In each of these places, regardless of whether the game was black bear, caribou, moose or white-tailed deer, the hunter was successful and pleased with the performance of his rifle.

PUMPING THE BENEFITS

Why a pump? Semiautos are faster for sure, but only if the goal is to make noise. For speed of follow-up shots, no action style even comes close to being as fast as a semiauto, but when shooting at a deer or any other target many hunters believe that a pump has the advantage.

The simple motion of pumping the gun helps speed up the follow-up shots. As the slide is brought back to eject the empty shell, it assists in bringing the gun down out of recoil, and as it is slammed forward with a fresh shell, it will bring the gun back on target. If the hunter keeps his eyes on the target as he works the action, the motion of slamming the slide forward will naturally bring the barrel and the sights back into alignment with where he's looking. For aimed,

repeated fire, most experienced shooters will agree that the pump is faster than any other rifle style.

When hunting thick country, this is an important feature in a rifle. Often the shots you must take are fleeting as the targets are running through dense brush. It's hard to make every shot count, so a speedy second, third or even fourth shot is often important. Of course, the goal is to hit the critter with the first shot, but reality is often something entirely different. When it takes more than one shot, the speed at which you can aim and fire those shots is crucial to your success.

With the ice, snow, mud and cold of deer hunting in the north country, a pump has the advantage over a semiauto. It is simply more reliable because it is manually operated, and a pump is easier to open and clean when it is covered with ice or full of mud from a fall.

The Remington 7600 has been the only big game pump action rifle on the market since Savage stopped production on the Model 170 in 1981. It has always been the only pump action rifle made in modern big game calibers, as the Savage was only chambered in .35 Remington and .30-30 Winchester.

WHAT'S AVAILABLE

The Remington has come through several generations to arrive at today's Model 7600. Currently, it is chambered in .243 Winchester, .270 Winchester, .280 Remington, .308 Winchester and .30-06 Springfield, and available with a wood or synthetic stock and forend.

The removable clip holds four rounds. The bolt locks up by rotating four forward lugs, similar to a bolt action, which allows the use of high-pressure modern cartridges. The barrel is completely free floating. In shooting a large variety of these rifles over the years, most with triggers that have been improved by a gunsmith, they have demonstrated the ability to produce outstanding hunting rifle accuracy.

In 1997, Browning decided to enter the pump action rifle market and they have advanced the program a little with even more powerful cartridges. The Browning Pump Rifle (BPR) is chambered in .243 Winchester, .308 Winchester, .270 Winchester, .30-06

For reliable and accurate repeat shots, most experienced hunters will agree that the pump is faster than any other rifle style.

After Savage stopped production on the Model 170 in 1981, the Remington 7600 survived as the only big game pump action rifle on the market. Then in 1997 Browning decided to enter the field with their elegant and powerful BPR (shown).

Springfield, 7mm Remington Magnum and .300 Winchester Magnum. The availability of magnum cartridges is an attraction to many shooters as this is certainly the only pump action rifle offered in such chamberings.

The removable box magazine is fitted into a swinging hinged floor plate, a very secure system that also protects the magazine from debris or damage. The rifle has a 22-inch barrel (magnum calibers have 24-inch tubes), an overall length of 43 inches and weighs about 7½ pounds. The trigger pull on mine is four pounds and breaks clean and crisp.

One unique feature is the way the forend pivots down as the slide is pulled back. The forend is long and comes back to cover the forward portion of the action. This doesn't leave a gap behind the forend as most pump guns have. While the aesthetic value is a matter of personal taste, there are some practical benefits in that dirt, sticks, leaves or other clutter are less likely to build up and hinder or jam the action. The bolt uses a seven forward lug rotating system for a positive lock up, and the barrel is completely free floating. My BPR has proven to be a very accurate rifle, shooting as well as many bolt-action rifles.

Pumps will never be a driving force in the marketplace, but they are one of the best selections you can make for some styles of hunting. I personally own several, and when I set out to build the ultimate eastern deer rifle a few years back, I chose a Remington 7600 in .35 Whelen for the foundation. I have had that rifle for more than a decade now, and even today I can't think of a way to improve on my original concept; for me it remains the ultimate woods rifle for whitetails. The reasons are many, but the fact that it's a pump action is primary.

Barrels, Stocks & Finishes

Rifle Barrel Length—What's Best for You?

I received my first lesson on the importance of barrel length when I was about 12 and still so new to hunting that green was rubbing off on everything I touched. One cold,

blustery and rainy November day, Dad, Uncle Butch and I pulled Dad's old Jeep into a grown-up field a couple of miles from our deer camp. Standing there was one of the biggest whitetail bucks on earth (at least I thought so at the time). In Butch's haste to get out, he grabbed Dad's long-barreled .30-06 instead of his own .38-55 carbine and, forgetting the difference in length, got the gun firmly wedged between the roof and the seat. In the short time it took to wrestle the gun free, the buck turned and walked back into the woods.

If Dad hadn't noticed that I had the hacksaw out of the toolbox that night, my own rifle might have been a carbine by morning. That was never going to happen to me!

In the three-plus decades of hunting since then, I have learned a little more about the importance of barrel length in rifles, not the least of which is that shorter is not always better. The best barrel length depends on a lot of factors, such as the cartridge used, the type of rifle, the terrain hunted, the type of shot expected and even the kind of hunter you are.

The reason for a longer barrel is to milk more velocity from the high-performance cartridges. The longer the burning powder has to push and accelerate the bullet, the higher the velocity will be. This assumes that the cartridge and powder are of a design that can utilize this longer barrel time. Some cartridges will burn all their powder in a short barrel, and some might benefit from an even longer barrel than is practical for hunting use.

Long Range: Long Barrel

With the increasing interest in long-range deer hunting, we are seeing a new class of cartridge emerge. Remington's 7mm STW and .300 Ultra Mag. as well as Weatherby's .30-378, are perfect examples. These cartridges feature a large powder capacity in relation to the bore diameter. They use vast amounts of slow-burning powder and need a long tube to work their high-velocity magic. Anything shorter than 26 inches or so and you are burning a lot of the powder outside of the barrel, where it makes an impressive flash but does nothing to increase velocity.

Even so-called "standard" magnums, such as the 7mm Rem. Mag. or the .300 Win. Mag., need at least 24 inches of pipe to perform up to expectations. Most rifles in these chamberings are shipped with that barrel length—and it works well for a general-purpose hunting rifle expected to be used under a variety of conditions—but a longer 26-inch tube will milk a little more velocity from the class of cartridges.

The mid-range cartridges such as the .30-06 and its many offspring are usually chambered in rifles with a 22-inch tube. While this provides the best balance between velocity and ergonomics for most shooters, there are exceptions. The new Weatherby Mark V Lightweight chambered in these calibers has a 24-inch barrel.

"Weatherby has always been performance-oriented," says Brad Ruddell, Vice President of Marketing. "In staying with that philosophy we decided to go with the longer barrels so that our rifles would produce a little more velocity with any given cartridge."

SHORTER IS OFTEN BETTER

The other end of the equation is in the shorter barrels favored by many hunters, particularly in the East. I have hunted Maine whitetails with the legendary Benoit family, and they have their guns custom designed for their style of hunting. They are trackers and are always on the move through the thick swamps and spruce-covered mountains of northern Maine. Their shots usually are close and often must be taken quickly at moving deer. This requires a short, light and fast-handling rifle, and the Benoits hunt exclusively with Remington pump action rifles with short barrels. They either buy the carbine model with an 18½-inch barrel or shorten the rifles to 19 inches.

Shorter-barrel guns are easier to get through the brush and are much quicker and more responsive when it's time to shoot fast. The short barrels point quickly and swing faster than longer barrels because the weight is closer to the shooter and there is less inertia to overcome when moving the rifle. Also, the end of the barrel being closer to the shooter's forward hand makes a shorter, more powerful arc, so the gun responds quicker. A shorter barrel is also that much less apt to tangle in the brush as the shooter tries to follow a running deer. With less barrel metal, the gun is simply lighter as well. That slight difference might not seem too important unless you are the person lugging it 15 miles a day.

While the heavy long barrels have a reputation for accuracy, it is a misconception to think that a short barrel is any less accurate. Actually, just the opposite is often the case. The stubby barrel is stiffer and accuracy is often enhanced.

Cartridges such as the .30-30 Win., .35 Rem. or .44 Rem. Mag. have less powder to burn and mate well with 20-inch tubes. They are used mostly in the thick woods, so the short gun is a benefit for all those previously mentioned reasons. Actually, some cartridges such as the .22 Long Rifle will lose velocity with a barrel much longer than 20 inches. Once the powder is burned there is no longer any thrust on the bullet and friction will cause it to slow.

Which cartridge works best with which barrel length is predicated on a lot of factors, but a basic rule of thumb is

Winchester Model 94 "Big-Bore" Black Shadow in .444 Marlin (left) and the Marlin 1895G Guide Gun in .45-70 (right) are two popular lever actions. The resurging popularity in these cartridges is being driven by hunters who prefer the feel and handling of a short barrel like the Guide rifle's.

How Does Barrel Length Affect Velocity?

The trade-off for a shorter barrel is a loss in velocity. With everything else being equal, in most cases, the longer the barrel, the faster the bullet will exit. Most references suggest that the loss with a shorter barrel will be 30- to 50-fps-per-inch of barrel. The problem is that it's not constant. Various cartridges will react differently, and even using another powder with the same cartridge can make a difference. The loss per inch also can escalate as the barrel length changes. A rifle might show a greater loss from 22 inches to 18 inches than it did between 26 inches and 22 inches, or vice versa. There is really no secret formula to determine how much.

I tested three .30-06 guns with different barrel lengths to see how much velocity difference there was between them. Using Remington 180-grain PSP Core-Lokt ammo, I fired strings with a Thompson Center TCR rifle with a 23-inch barrel, a Remington 7600 carbine with an 18.5-inch barrel and a Thompson Center Encore handgun with a 15-inch barrel. Velocity was measured with an Oehler 35P chronograph 10 feet from the muzzle.

The TCR averaged 2,644 fps, the Remington, 2,520 fps and the Encore, 2,353 fps. Between the two rifles, the difference was 124 fps, or about 27.5 fps per inch of barrel. The difference between the TCR and the handgun was 291 fps, or 36.4 fps per inch of barrel. Between the Remington and the Encore, the difference was 167 fps, or 47.7 fps per inch.

Note that the greatest per-inch difference occurred between the 18.5-inch barrel and the 15-inch barrel. Obviously something important was happening in that section of barrel.

However, another load in these same guns may produce different results. The only way to know for sure how big a velocity drop will occur is to shoot the gun and ammo across a good chronograph.

A general rule of thumb: With all else being equal, a shorter rifle barrel will produce less velocity. That is the case here with these Marlin .45-70 rifles, but many hunters will make the velocity sacrifice in order to have the faster-handling, short-barreled rifle.

that the more powder a cartridge uses, the longer the barrel it will need to perform efficiently. Sometimes, though, how and where you hunt will influence the barrel length suited for the task. It may be in your best interest to give up a little velocity for a gun that handles faster or carries easier.

STIFF RIFLE BARRELS

Rifles designed for long-range shooting also usually feature a heavy barrel. The stiffer barrel is also less reactive to barrel vibrations when firing, so it's usually inherently more accurate than a thin barrel. These guns are designed to be

Most long range rifles such as this Remington Model 700 Sendero will have a stiff, heavy barrel to minimize the effect of harmonic vibrations and enhance accuracy.

fired from a rest of some kind, and the additional weight out front helps the gun settle down and allows for more precise holding for long-range shooting. The more mass weight in a gun, the less it will react to influences such as wind or even the shooter's heartbeat. It is much easier to steady a heavy-barreled, 10-pound rifle than it is a 6-pound ultra-light.

SYNTHETIC & LAMINATED STOCKS

The gun industry is conservative and slow to embrace change. For example, from sometime around the first reference to firearms in 1326 until very recently, wood was the primary substance used in gun handles and stocks.

It was only a little more than a decade ago that we first started seeing synthetic stocks on hunting rifles. They caught on, though, and according to an informal survey I conducted of the major rifle makers, about half of the rifles they ship now have synthetic stocks.

More than a few rifles that leave the factory fitted with wood soon find replacements with an aftermarket stock. Either way, it seems that wood in its natural form is, after seven centuries, falling from grace as a material for stocks on hunting rifles.

By now it's common knowledge with most hunters that the problem with wood is that moisture causes the wood

Today's serious hunting rifle is usually equipped with either a laminated wood or a synthetic stock. These stocks are inert to moisture and are usually stronger than wood.

fibers to swell, changing the dimensions of the stock, which can cause the stock to warp. This will result in accuracy problems as well as point-of-impact shifts. Synthetic stocks are inert to moisture. They are also usually stronger than wood, and when they're damaged, they are easily repaired. Some manufacturers claim they're much lighter, but that is not usually the case except in the very expensive fiberglass or Kevlar stocks. However, from a purely pragmatic aspect, synthetic stocks are superior in every way to wood.

One of the big reasons wood was used for gun stocks all those years was aesthetics. To the eyes of a lot of hunters, particularly traditionalists, synthetic stocks are just plain ugly. There are a lot of hunters who believe that a rifle just doesn't look right unless it's wearing furniture made of wood, and there is no denying that wood does somehow look "right" on a rifle. Wood also has a certain feel that no synthetic can replace.

With that in mind, another alternative is to consider a wood-laminate stock. These stocks offer the inert weather-proofing of synthetic with likely even more strength, while maintaining the warmth and feel of wood. The downside is that they are a bit heavier than the other stocks.

Perhaps it's time you left the 14th century and considered a wood-laminate or synthetic stock on your next gun.

STAINLESS STEEL VS. CARBON STEEL

If you will forgive the cliché, the stainless steel rifle has taken the hunting world by storm. These rifles are a pragmatic answer to the problems of a hard-working hunting rifle because the metal requires less attention during a foul-weather hunt. Stainless steel guns are so well infiltrated into the big-game hunting world today that it is hard to believe it was

The three most popular choices for rifle stocks are (top to bottom): laminated wood, synthetic and wood. Laminated and synthetic stocks are replacing traditional wood as the material of choice for hunting rifles.

only in 1988 that Browning was the first major gun company to offer this type of rifle.

Today, Remington and Ruger say that about half their sales of bolt-action hunting rifles are in stainless steel.

One attraction is that maintenance is less important, but the gun will still rust. However, when it's impossible to give the rifle the attention it deserves, there is no question that stainless steel buys a lot of forgiveness.

They are not, however, without their critics. Stainless steel is tougher to machine, so the cost is higher when buying the rifle. It often also means as a rule that the parts are not quite as polished and smooth in a stainless steel gun. It has been my experience that on the average, a factory-grade stainless steel rifle will not shoot quite as accurately as its carbon or blued steel counterpart. I attribute that to the difficulty of working with stainless steel and the slightly less polished surfaces that result.

The differences, though, are small and academic at best. Almost any new rifle today will shoot astonishingly well, regardless of the type of steel used. If the stainless steel models average groups of 1½ inches instead of the 1¼ inches with carbon steel, so what?

The other downside of stainless steel rifles is that even with a bead-blasted matte finish, they are more visible. In the past decade, I have watched a lot of other hunters with rifles in the fields and woods. The color and reflective nature of stainless steel make the guns much more noticeable than

blued rifles, particularly those with a matte blue finish. I can't say I know of specific instances where it has spooked game, but I certainly notice a stainless steel gun more in the field. Often, when the hunter is wearing camo, his rifle barrel is the first thing I notice.

All that said, these days I use stainless steel rifles while hunting as much as, or more than, blued guns because they're tougher and easier to maintain.

SHINY RIFLES

Although they have fallen from grace in recent years, highly polished rifles still have market appeal. They may be pretty to look at, but they are not well suited for hunting.

The best illustration of this I have seen was when a friend and I were hunting whitetails in Alberta. My buddy Russ Tarbell had bought a new rifle for the trip from a highly regarded rifle maker. It might easily have been called a work of art. The stock was well-figured walnut with fine checkering and a gloss finish his wife could check her makeup in. The metal was polished in a blue so deep you could see yesterday hiding in the depths. I commented more than once that it was "too pretty to hunt with." I thought I was just busting his chops a bit; I didn't realize how true that statement would prove to be.

The outfitter put Russ in a treestand along a big wheat field where he had been seeing a huge buck. After three days

Stainless steel rifles with synthetic stocks are a pragmatic answer to the problems of a hard-working hunting rifle. The metal requires less attention during a foul-weather hunt, and moisture will not affect the stock.

Russ was getting frustrated.

"I don't understand it," he said. "Every morning I can see deer coming, but they get to that hill about 200 yards from me and they stop, stare and go the other way."

We solved the mystery the next morning as we sat on a distant hill with a powerful spotting scope. It was like Russ was waving a mirror up in that tree. Every time he moved, or the wind blew (which it does a lot in Alberta) and the tree moved, the rifle flashed like he was shipwrecked and trying to signal passing airplanes. We went down to where the deer had been spotting him from, and it was, if anything, even more apparent.

Some steel wool and determined elbow grease solved the problem until we could get home and turn the rifle over to a gunsmith for total refinishing.

I must admit, though, to shedding a tear or two while they scrubbed away. It really was a very pretty rifle.

Today, stainless steel guns are so well infiltrated into the big game hunting world, it is hard to believe that the big gun companies first began to offer this type of rifle as recently as the late 1980s.

Chapter 2

HUNTING RIFLES & CARTRIDGES

egarding the evolution of rifle ammunition, we have come a long way since Roger Bacon introduced the Western world to gunpowder back in 1248. The matchlock passed the torch to the wheel lock. From that evolved the flintlock and on to the percussion rifle, and then the invention of self-contained cartridges. Gone was the need for loading separate components in several steps. No longer did a shooter need to measure each charge. A large supply of ammunition could be carried ready for use and it could be waterproofed, so weather became a less inhibiting problem. Self-contained cartridges also greatly decreased reloading time.

The centerfire of the 19th century evolved from blackpowder and corrosive priming to modern calibers with small-caliber, high-velocity jacketed bullets. Incidentally, the first commercial cartridge to use this concept made possible by smokeless powders was none other than the .30-30 Win. It was introduced in 1895 along with the .25-35 Win. in the Winchester Model 1894 rifle as the first commercial hunting cartridge and rifle designed specifically to use the "new-fangled" smokeless powder.

To this day, with further evolution in cartridge design and in smokeless powders, velocities continue to increase, and new bullet technological advancements ensure that terminal performance keeps pace. When we look back at the changes in hunting guns over the past 200 years, the advances are awe-inspiring.

TOP 10 CARTRIDGES

ased on recent sales information from the big three ammo makers and from RCBS reloading dies, here are the top 10 rifle cartridges.

#1: .30-06 Springfield
Unquestionably the reigning king, this cartridge was listed first by all except Federal, who had it as number two.

The .30-06 Springfield was adopted by the government as a military round in 1906. It featured a few design changes from its predecessor, the .30-03, along with a lighter bullet than the .30-03's 220-grain. Success as a sporting round was almost a foregone conclusion because the .30-06 may well be the most versatile cartridge in existence for North American big-game hunting. With 125-grain bullets, it is suitable for varmint hunting. The 150-grain bullet shoots flat enough for pronghorns and Western deer hunting. With 165-grain bullets, it may well be the perfect deer cartridge. Moving up to 180-grain bullets, it becomes a viable elk and moose cartridge, particularly when using premium bullets. While the .30-06 is light for dangerous bears, it has taken more than a few over the years. Here, a 200-grain premium bullet is the way to go; however, since none of the majors currently load this weight, handloads are necessary.

#2: .223 Remington
The .223 Rem. first appeared in 1957 as the 5.56mm NATO. The 5.56mm NATO was adopted by the military in February 1964 and by the sporting public as the .223 Rem. one month later.

This round probably sees a more diverse listing of uses than any other ammo currently manufactured. It continues use as a military round and is popular with civilian shooters of the AR-15 and other quasi-military semiauto rifles. It is highly favored for shooting prairie dogs, gophers and ground squirrels because of its accuracy, flat trajectory and mild recoil. It will kill tough coyotes and is usually not too destructive of the fur, even on foxes and bobcats.

Finally, the Service Rifle category of the National Match course is usually fired with a .223 Rem. in an AR-15 type rifle.

Popular factory loads feature bullet weights from 40 grains to 75 grains. The heavier bullets are best left to target shooting with specialized rifles, while the 55-grain bullets work well on tough predators like the coyote. The 50- to 53-grain bullets are good for most hunting, but a lot of shooters are building an attachment to the fast 40-grain loads, such as Winchester's new Ballistic Silvertip.

#3: .270 Winchester
When the .270 was introduced by Winchester in 1925, it was pretty hot stuff; it still is, even today. The origins of this oddball bullet diameter are a bit murky, and without high praise from Jack O'Connor, the .270 Win. might have found itself as a listing in the obsolete cartridge section of most references. Instead, it is one of the most successful "modern" cartridges ever designed.

The bullet most often associated with the .270 is the 130-grain. With this, the .270 Win. is a great long-range cartridge for pronghorns, deer and even sheep. Many hunters, though, prefer the heavier 140- and 150-grain loads. While the .270 is pretty light for elk or moose, it does see use on these critters.

#4: .30-30 Winchester
It's old, antiquated, underpowered, poorly designed and simply past its time, but guess what—the old "thirty-thirty" outsells most of the so-called modern cartridges by a wide margin.

Everybody knows that the modern bottlenecked, high-velocity cartridges have replaced the big straight-walled blackpowder cartridges of the last century as the choice for serious hunters. What most fail to realize is that when the .30-30 Win. was introduced in 1895, it was the cartridge that led that revolution. It was the first sporting cartridge to use the new-fangled smokeless powder and little bullets at high (relatively speaking) speeds.

The .30-30 Win. is a deer cartridge, pure and simple. It

wasn't made for varmints, it's not big enough for elk or moose and using it on dangerous game can kill you. But as a deer cartridge, it has probably made more venison than any other cartridge in history.

Current factory loads are 150 or 170 grains, although Federal lists a 125-grain load.

#5: .308 Winchester

The .308 was introduced by Winchester in 1952 while the military adopted it as the 7.62 x 51mm NATO in 1954.

Think of this as the .30-06's little brother. It's a half-inch shorter, but it works hard to keep up and factory velocities run only about 100 fps behind the '06, mostly because the .308 Win. is loaded to slightly higher pressures.

Its biggest asset for the hunter is that the .308 Win. will fit in short-action rifles, which are shorter and lighter. The .308 Win. will do almost everything a .30-06 can do when using lighter bullets, but when the heavy pills are loaded, the lesser case capacity makes the gap start to grow. It is a great deer cartridge, and popular bullet weights run from 150 to 180 grains.

#6: .243 Winchester

In 1955 Winchester necked down its .308 to 6mm and created the .243 Win. Its primary competition was the 6mm Rem. and the .250 Sav.; they both lost the race.

The .243 Win. is often touted as a "dual-use" cartridge, that is, a varmint gun that works for deer, or vice versa. With good 100-grain bullets, it is a pretty good deer cartridge if its limitations are understood and adhered to religiously. With lighter bullets, it is an outstanding coyote gun with little or no compromise. For prairie dogs and the like, it may have a little more recoil than the .22 centerfires, but it bucks the wind better and so becomes a shooter's choice.

Bullet weights range from 55 grains to 105 grains.

#7: 7mm Remington Magnum

By far the most popular of the belted magnums, the 7mm Rem. Mag. was introduced in 1962. It offers a flat-shooting, hard-hitting cartridge with recoil levels that most shooters can endure. In the hunting field, it is in the same class as the .30-06, and anything that can be said of that cartridge applies to the 7mm Rem. Mag. With 140- to 150-grain bullets, it is great for deer, pronghorns, sheep, etc. For moose or elk, use

175-grain premium bullets. The big bears can be taken with this cartridge, but it's not the best choice.

#8: .300 Winchester Magnum

Winchester introduced its medium-bore belted magnum in 1963.

If I could have one rifle for hunting in North America, it would be a .300 Win. It may not be quite as popular as the 7mm Rem. Mag., primarily because it kicks quite a bit more, but for those who can handle the recoil, it offers a lot more versatility. Bullets from 150- to 165-grain shoot flat for pronghorns, deer, sheep and goats, while the 180-grain bullets work great on tough trophy deer and black bears. The 200-grain loads are perfect for elk and moose and even the nasty bears of the northcountry.

#9: .22-250 Remington

The .22-250 Rem. is likely the most popular long-range varmint round in common use today. It is a well-behaved but high-powered varmint cartridge that is inherently accurate and shoots very fast and very flat. It was created by necking the .250-3000 Sav. down to .22 caliber. The parent cartridge was introduced in 1915, and it is thought that the .22-250 wildcat appeared shortly after that. Remington domesticated it in 1965 as a factory load.

The 50- to 53-grain bullet weight range is the most practical; however, the heavier 55-grain has a strong following, particularly with coyote hunters. But if it's speed you crave, a 40-grain bullet can easily be pushed past the magic 4,000 fps mark from most rifles. Federal lists it right at 4,000 fps in their catalog. Hornady and Winchester list it at 4,150 fps.

#10: Take your pick! This is the one that nobody could agree on and there was no overlap. Federal has the .30 Carbine as its number eight best seller. RCBS has the .25-06 Rem. in tenth place, Winchester places the .22 Hornet in its number five slot and Remington lists the .222 Rem. in ninth place.

DEER GUNS EAST

"Oh, East is East and West is West, and never the twain shall meet, Till Earth and sky stand presently at God's great Judgment seat."
                                                        —*Rudyard Kipling*

Could Kipling have been wrong?

Not judging from where I was standing. My boots were in the same tracks I had occupied when the shooting started, and I was looking at my bright red daypack sitting on the spot where the deer had stood.

I had been slowly still-hunting, working the transition line about halfway up the mountain between the evergreens and the hard woods. I topped a small ridge, and in one of

those magic times that every hunter experiences now and then, he was just there.

Now I question how I could have seen him. Currently, I was looking at a bright patch of red backpack that I knew was there, but the brush was so thick that I could barely make it out. When the buck and I made eye contact, he knew he was in trouble and had gone ballistic. It took three very fast shots (well, one of them actually killed a maple), but he was down there beside my backpack while I was poking in the snow looking for my brass. (If you are a handloader, then you understand.)

I'd had a good string of one-shot kills going up until that moment, but I had made the fatal mistake of bragging about it. This was, I suppose, the hunting gods' way of humbling me.

Surprisingly, though, that's not what I was thinking about as I trudged on home with the whitetail faithfully following my drag rope. True to "gun crank" doctrine, I was pondering on how different East and West deer hunting could be and how different the demands were on the rifles we use.

"Brush Guns"

There are exceptions to every rule, and for the sake of clarity, I consider an Eastern rifle one that is designed to handle fast and shoot well in thick brush, where shots are expected to be close.

Whitetail hunting in the East has long been the traditional home for short, fat cartridges with large-diameter, blunt bullets,

but they are falling from favor these days. Hunters have long since realized that the so-called "modern" calibers with bottleneck cartridge design and pointed bullets driven to high velocities can do anything at 50 yards that they can do at 250—and do it better. With the trend away from traditional mobile hunting methods and to treestands or other stationary methods, the demands of an Eastern hunter's rifle are changing. Hunters today walk less and shoot at fewer running deer.

That's not to say that we should simply forget all of the old traditional calibers. Everything that they have been doing for generations they continue to do and now do it better, regardless of whether they are fired from a treestand or by a moving still-hunter. Their performance has improved because of new powders, better bullet designs and higher-quality guns.

These blunt, heavy bullets have always had a reputation for "hammering" game, and it is well deserved. The frontal area of many of the traditional calibers is already larger than that of some modern bullets after expansion. Couple this with the excellent expansion qualities of most of these bullets, and you can understand that "hammering" is an accurate analogy.

It still remains true in much of the Northeast that traditional deer hunting means covering some country. Tracking, still-hunting and other popular methods will take the hunter over a

I'd had a good string of one-shot kills going before this deer but had made the mistake of bragging about it. This buck took three very fast shots; two hit him while one wounded a maple tree.

lot of ground in a day, ground that can often be rugged and steep. While these methods have proven successful for taking deer, the resulting shots are often at running deer in thick woods. For these hunters, ease of carrying and the handling qualities while shooting at game are stronger influencing factors than ballistic efficiency. Because the ranges are usually short, any hunter who prefers the delightful carrying and handling characteristics of the traditional brush rifles, such as a lever action, pump action or semiauto, shouldn't feel handicapped in the least. Consider too that some of today's light bolt actions, such as Remington's Model Seven, are gaining popularity with woods hunters for many of the same reasons.

CALIBERS & CARTRIDGES

When it comes to cartridges, the .24 calibers are considered by many, including me, to be the minimum for deer. But while other writers speak eloquently of the .24's long-range capabilities, I categorize the .243 Win. and 6mm Rem. to be

short- to moderate-range deer rifles. They simply run out of steam too fast to be reliable on deer at long range. With good 100-grain bullets, they are decent enough deer cartridges if the deer are not too big or the ranges not too long. I would not use a .243 to shoot deer beyond 250 yards, and I certainly would not select one to hunt the big trophy bucks of western Canada. But for the mythical "average" deer shot in the woods at relatively close range, they do a fine job. (I know this because years ago, before I became "enlightened" about ballistics, I shot a lot of deer with a .243 Win. Just to remind me, my two kids took seven deer between them last year. Six of them fell to .243 Wins. For the record, the other one was taken with a muzzleloader.)

Any larger bullet is fine, of course, provided that it has a combination of enough bullet weight and velocity at the point of impact. The .30 carbine is not a deer caliber, and although some will dispute it, neither is the 7.62 X 39. If a medium caliber lacks velocity, then it must have bullet weight. If both are missing, then it's just not a deer gun.

The handling qualities of the rifle are often as important as the cartridge for Eastern hunting. Some of today's light bolt actions, like this Weatherby Mark V Lightweight, are gaining popularity with woods hunters.

In the thick woods of the Northeast, whitetail hunting often means fast shooting at running bucks. Many hunters prefer a short, quick and powerful rifle like this Remington 7600 pump action carbine in .30-06.

In the so-called short-action "modern" calibers, deer guns start with the .243 Win. and include the .260 Rem., 7mm-08 Rem. and .308 Win.

Just about all the long-action calibers from the .25-06 Rem. on up through the .300 Mag. are well suited for Eastern whitetails. Deer are really not that big or hard to kill, and any of these cartridges, when loaded with quality bullets, hit more than hard enough at short ranges in the woods.

With the traditional calibers shooting slow-moving, flat-nosed bullets, a hunter will be well advised to stay with 7mm and larger. But remember that these cartridges built their reputation with big bullets. When chambered for light, quick-handling rifles, calibers like the .444 Marlin, .375 Win. and even the .44 Rem. Mag. are deadly on whitetails at short range. From .30-30 Win. to .45-70 Gov., these cartridges have been making venison for years and will continue to do so if you do your part. Your part consists of keeping the range short and the shot placed correctly.

A CONCLUSION

It's often the handling qualities of the rifle as much as the cartridge that are important for brush guns. For the deer I mentioned at the beginning of this chapter, I had to shoot fast. I was using an old and faithful Remington 760 pump in .30-06. It fits me like a grouse gun and always feels responsive and alive in my hands. It was that more than my selection of caliber that allowed me to tag that buck.

These are but a few of the examples of cartridges used for hunting white-tailed deer in the East, representing the diversity of those cartridges that work well there. Pictured (left to right): .270 Win., 7-30 Waters, .308 Win., .35 Rem., .356 Win. and .45-70 Gov.

ONE DEER (AND MORE) GUN

Consider, if you will, if it became a reality for reasons economic or social that you could have only one deer rifle. Which one would work best under the most diverse conditions?

The average deer hunter lives and hunts in the East. Most of us dream of the trip we will make "out West" someday to hunt the giant whitetails that live in the open spaces there, or mule deer up in the mountains or out in the breaks. We might also plan an elk hunt and maybe consider moose, caribou or pronghorns. Is there one rifle that can handle all of this? It's a tall order, but yes, there is.

ACTION: BOLT

You may be subjecting this gun to some harsh conditions in the years ahead, and when it is crusted over with a mixture of ice, leaves and dirt, the bolt gun is more reliable by design than any other. That alone is reason enough to choose one. Which bolt action is up to you. I have tried most, and I have my preferences. They are, however, based on personal biases and not necessarily performance since any of the better bolt guns can and will shoot extremely well.

CALIBER: .30-06

A flat-shooting and accurate caliber is important, one with versatility and the option of heavy bullets. The plain vanilla .30-06 might not be glamorous, but it has been getting the job done since 1906, and with today's bullets and powders it's doing it better than ever. When using my pet load with a Speer 165-grain Spitzer and the gun sighted for 200 yards, it's only 1.8 inches high at 100 yards and 7.7 inches low at 300. So that basically means I can hold on a deer at any reasonable distance and kill it cleanly.

The .30-06 Springfield is likely your best choice if you can only have one gun for hunting whitetails and other big game.

BULLETS: I'LL GIVE YOU A COUPLE

There are some wonderful 180-grain and 200-grain bullets available for elk or moose, and with 150-grain bullets at 2,900 fps, the '06 becomes a great antelope rifle. On deer, the .30-06's effectiveness is unquestioned at any range.

PRONGHORNS & LONG-RANGE DEER

When it comes to selecting cartridges for hunting the wide-open spaces, deer and pronghorn hunting have a lot in common. The key is selecting a cartridge that will shoot flat to assist in reaching out across those empty lands. To achieve that, the bullet should exit the rifle with a velocity at or very near 3,000 fps. It goes without saying that the bullet should have a streamlined shape and a high ballistic coefficient. It should also have good terminal ballistic qualities to ensure that it will expand well at the lower-impact velocity of long shots and still hold together on the closer hits where it's going much faster.

YOU NEED ENOUGH ENERGY

The difference in critters is that big trophy deer, particularly mule deer, are much bigger and tougher than the most macho pronghorns that ever grazed the plains. The long-held standard of energy for deer hunting has been 1,000 foot-pounds (fp) delivered at the target. That's acceptable for pronghorns and most deer. However, with today's dwindling hunting opportunities and the limited time that most of us have to hunt, I would put the threshold higher for deer.

There seems to be more emphasis placed on trophy quality today than in generations past, and trophy bucks are different from their little brothers. These are the biggest, toughest deer in the herd. They

Hunting in the wide open spaces of the Great Plains can result in long shots at big game. An accurate, flat shooting rifle is but one requirement; the hunter must also have the skill to make a long shot.

Long-range hunting for deer and antelope requires accurate rifles and flat shooting cartridges. The Remington's heavy barrel helps it shoot more accurately, while the cartridge's high velocity flattens the bullet's trajectory.

know they are dominant and they act it; they fear little and feel inferior to nothing. They are at their peak of physical conditioning and have proven their dominance in battle. They have a tenacity to life that stretches beyond that of most other deer. It is always best to plan on the worst-case scenario with trophy bucks and to err a little on the side of more power. For these deer, I draw the bottom line at 1,500 fp delivered at the target.

I also think that a genuine 300 yards is a very long shot and is as far as most of us should consider shooting at game. I'll allow a cushion for the recognition that most of us will stretch that now and again, particularly if the antlers or horns are big. So the cartridge must be able to deliver that energy to 400 yards.

THE .200 FAMILY, PLUS 6 & 7MMS

The only 6mm cartridge that honestly meets the 1,000 fp pronghorn requirement is the .240 Wthby Mag. Both the 6mm Rem. and the .243 Win. poop out early. If you absolutely keep your shots to less than 300 yards, they work, but will you?

The .25-06 Rem. makes the cut, but barely. The .257 Wthby Mag. does it a little better. The .260 Rem. will slide in, but only if long barrels are used and the factory-published ballistics are honest. My testing so far says they are not. The .264 Win. may be one of the finest pronghorn rifles ever conceived, but who uses one today? I don't think any gun company is making them. The .264 is often called a belted

.270 Win., and every gun company on earth makes rifles for this cartridge. With sleek 130-grain bullets, it's a great pronghorn cartridge. The .270 Wthby Mag. does it even better because it's faster. The .270 Win. doesn't make the cut for trophy deer, although it's close. I expect I'll take some nasty hits from .270 fans for pointing out its inadequacies, but the facts are inarguable. Based on factory specs, the .270 Wthby Mag. does it for deer with room to spare.

You might consider the 7mm-08 Rem., but in this scenario I see little use for any short-action cartridge. Bullets heavy enough for hunting big game—that is, 140 grains or more—fall far short of 3,000 fps from any factory short-action cartridge and the guns commonly used to shoot them. So even if the energy is acceptable, the velocity is such that the trajectory arch is a little too big for good long-range shooting.

The .280 Rem. is a far better choice. It's also just slipping into the domain of our long-range trophy deer cartridge. With the right loads and rifle, where a 140-grain bullet is hitting an honest 3,000 fps, it carries our 1,500 fp energy threshold past 400 yards (although I have yet to see that velocity on my chronograph screen from a 140-grain factory load fired from a .280 Rem. with a 22-inch barrel). Some handloads will do it, but my personal solution was to have one of my .280 Rems. rechambered to .280 Ackley Improved. It now easily pushes a 140-grain Nosler Ballistic Tip bullet to 3,100 fps from a 22-inch barrel.

The 7mm Rem. Mag., 7mm Wthby Mag. and 7mm STW all do it nicely with bullets from 140 to 160 grains. They are excellent choices for deer or pronghorns. Remember that there is no such thing as overkill; you can't make something too dead. The one constant in this style of hunting is the always-present possibility of a very long shot. The flatter a rifle cartridge will shoot, the better pronghorn or long-range deer gun it becomes. Flat trajectories always require high velocity. A by-product of high velocity with a hunting-weight bullet is energy. Energy grows exponentially to velocity, so the gains in energy are always larger than the increases in velocity. If a bullet that shoots flat delivers much more than the needed

Left to right: .308 Win., .30-06 Springfield, .300 Win., .300 Wthby, 7mm Wthby, 7mm Rem. Mag., .280 Rem. and 7mm-08 Rem. For long-range deer and antelope hunting, flat trajectory is important. The cartridges in the center of this lineup shoot faster, and therefore flatter, than those on the outside and are much better selections for this kind of hunting.

energy, so what? Dead is dead, but you've got to hit them first!

THE .300 FAMILY

The .308 Win. has that "short-action syndrome" mentioned earlier. It carries enough energy for pronghorns, but trajectories are a little arched. The .30-06 barely makes the cut for trophy deer. You must use a bullet with a high ballistic coefficient to hold the energy up. The hot factory loads with Nosler 165-grain Ballistic Tip bullets or the Federal load with Sierra boattail bullets would be among my first choices.

The .300 magnums all are flat shooting and hard hitting. The .300 Win. Mag., .300 Wthby Mag. and even the big .300 Rem. Ultra Mag. and .30-378 Wthby Mag. will deliver a bullet with all our requirements. The downside is that excessive recoil is starting to rear its ugly head. Some shooters find that once the .30 caliber magnum threshold is crossed, recoil becomes hard to manage. It is far better to be honest with yourself and choose a rifle with slightly less power if you are recoil shy. The primary importance in any long-range hunting situation is that you be able to shoot the rifle well. On the other hand, if you are indeed able to shoot well, the magnums are all outstanding for long-range hunting.

Moving up from there is unnecessary. There are some bigger cartridges that will work—the .340 Wthby Mag., .338-378 Wthby, .338 Win. Mag. and Remington's .338 Ultra Mag. all fit the bill. But they kick! Recoil starts to become a dominating factor with any shooter. Long-range hunting requires precision shooting, and it's a very rare individual who can do his or her best with these cartridges from hunting-weight rifles. Besides, while it's true that there is no such thing as overkill, there is a line of absurdity. For pronghorns and even deer, these big guns start to cross it.

BEAR GUNS

"*I* do not know that I have had many interesting experiences, unless you include bear hunting on the list."
—*Theodore Roosevelt*

It looked like a big black basketball gliding along the tops of the high goldenrod that grew in this abandoned log landing. But as it emerged into the edge of the woods, there formed like an apparition a large black body under the giant head. There was no clue to alert the bear that I was there and aiming a rifle at him, but when he turned to look at me, his eyes said he knew. I saw the muscles in his shoulder bunch to flee just as I pulled the trigger. Then, faster than I thought possible, he was gone.

I waited a few minutes for my eyes to adjust to the dim light before starting to track him. The trail soon led to a sharp drop-off, and as I crept up to that bank, intent on the land beyond, I almost stepped on him. He was just over the lip, facing back, watching for me.

I have shot many bears since then, but none larger, and I often wonder if he was lying in ambush and simply died before I got there. There is no way to know, of course, but regardless, I was glad I was using enough gun that night. The shot was far from perfect, hitting his liver. I question,

Really Big Bears

Grizzly and brown bears are one and the same from a scientific standpoint. It's just that the coastal brown bear lives an easier life and over the years has evolved into a bigger bear. Based on weights, a grizzly is about twice as big as a black bear, and a brown is three times as big. Polar bears are about the same as the brown bear in weight.

All these bears share a common bond in that they are North America's only true dangerous big game. They have the ability, disposition, tools and willingness to kill you. It would serve you well to keep that in mind when selecting a rifle to hunt the big bears.

From the standpoint of what to shoot them with, we can consider these bears as all alike. They are big, tough, nasty tempered and hard to kill. If you hunt them, it will be expensive, and it's unlikely that you will ever do much of it in your lifetime. You owe it to yourself and to the bear to show up well equipped.

The minimum gun suggested in most texts is a .300 magnum with 200-grain bullets. I don't know about you, but if I were facing 1,000 pounds of raging teeth and claws, .30 caliber would seem pretty puny no matter what the bullet weight.

A .338 Win. Mag. with 250-grain bullets seems like a more prudent minimum to my thinking. Better still, consider the .340 Wthby Mag., .338-378 Wthby Mag. or .338 Rem. Ultra Mag. The .375 H&H Mag. with 270- to 300-grain bullets seems about right, and the .378 Wthby Mag. doesn't look like too much gun to me. Any of the .416 rifles with 400-grain bullets would make decent shooters for big bears.

While many guides carry .458 Win., it's not really a bear-hunting cartridge. Guides usually don't bring their rifles into action until things have turned sour. That means they aren't shooting until the bear is too close. When you are hunting, it's foolish to shoot at a bear that's a long way away from you, but with a good rifle a 250-yard shot is reasonable. The .458 Win. is not really a 250-yard gun.

When a bear is big enough to leave a track this size, no rifle will make you feel over gunned. This grizzly bear track dwarfs a .338 Winchester shell.

When facing 1,000 pounds of teeth and claws with the attitude of a pro wrestler in a rage, any bear hunter will be glad he decided to pack a big gun.

---

might he still have been alive when I found him if I had been using a lesser cartridge than that 7mm Mag.?

DEER GUNS ARE NOT BEAR GUNS

It is often said that any gun that works for deer is fine for bears. Don't you believe it. It takes a lot more gun to reliably kill black bears than it does to kill white-tailed deer. Bears are a lot different from deer, with thicker hides, bigger bones, bulkier muscles and an inherent toughness that deer simply don't possess. When a deer is hurt, it's a sure bet that he will lie down before too long. A bear takes off with a destination in mind; he will either get to that place or die trying. I have tracked dozens of wounded bears, and those I have found have either been dead or in a damn good hiding place. I have never found one still alive that was bedded in the open.

Certainly, many calibers will kill bears, but that doesn't necessarily make them good bear guns. A bear gun should remove any doubt; it should not simply be adequate but should be as suited for the worst-case scenario as it is for the best. With bears, that can involve a lot of factors, not the least of which is the bear himself. I have weighed a lot of black bears, and most are a lot smaller than people think. The majority of the 500-pound bears you hear about never get near a scale. If there is a critter that is harder to drag than a black bear, it has escaped my notice. They pull like they are extracting one last revenge, and a bear will make you earn every foot you gain toward the truck. At the end, they all are 500 pounds to the guys that pulled them out.

Sure, some places consistently produce larger averages, but the truth is that the majority of the black bears shot are less than 250 pounds after field dressing. Most are under 200 pounds. The wild card is the bear that can show up no matter where you are hunting that does weigh an honest 350 or even 500 pounds. Those are a completely different critter, and if you plan your cartridge choice around the mythical "average" bear, you might be in for a sad surprise if you run into one of these big bruins.

CONSIDER HOW YOU'LL BE HUNTING

Another big factor is hunting style. Hunting over bait or with hounds will give you much closer shots than spot-and-stalk or hunting crop fields. This is a consideration in cartridge selection. For example, I favor a handloaded .45-70 Gov. for bait hunting. Its big, heavy bullet is a bear thumper that puts them down with authority. But it would be a poor choice for a spot-and-stalk hunt where the shots may be 200 yards or more; a .300 or .338 Win. Mag. might be a better choice.

But remember too that anything the .300 or .338 Win. Mag. can do at long range it can do even better up close. So there is no real downside from a ballistic standpoint to using these cartridges for any bear hunt; a 250-grain bullet from a .338 Win. Mag. is even more deadly on close bears over bait than it is on those long shots.

The consideration may be in the rifles chambered. A 9½-pound magnum with a 26-inch barrel is a gun you will hate personally after lugging it for a few grueling days spent chasing hounds. It would be far better to carry a slick little iron-sighted carbine chambered for .356 Win., .444 Marlin or .45-70 Gov. and weighing only 6½ pounds.

In places where calling bears is a common hunting tactic

Bear hunting is no time to fool around with marginal cartridges. It's always a good idea to hit bears with big bullets. Bear guns (left to right): Winchester M-70 .375 H&H, Savage Kodiak .338 Winchester and Marlin 1895 SS .45-70 Government. They all hit hard and anchor bears quickly.

With proper bullets, these are all good bear cartridges. They are all powerful enough to take any black bear. All but the .45-70 will reach out for long range shots as well. Left to right: 7mm Remington Magnum, 7mm Weatherby, 7mm STW, .30-06 Springfield, .300 Winchester, .300 Weatherby, .30-378 Weatherby, .338 Winchester, .340 Weatherby, .35 Whelen, .375 H&H & .45-70 Government.

it is said that the bears often come in very aggressively. This is a different bear than one that may be placidly feeding, and it sometimes takes a lot of killing with these pumped-up beasts. It's no place to fool with marginal calibers, and the people who hunt this way favor big guns with quality bullets.

THE QUESTION OF CALIBER

Any bear you shoot should have a hole on both sides. Forget that nonsense about leaving the bullet in the bear and expending all its energy. You need an exit hole for lots of reasons, but the primary one is because bears are notoriously hard to track. Their feet are wide, flat and soft, so they will leave few followable tracks on most ground. Their hair soaks up a lot of blood, and bullet holes are quick to plug up with fat and tissue. The best insurance is to use a large enough cartridge with a high-quality bullet that is on the heavy side for the caliber so that it will exit, leaving a large enough hole for a decent blood trail.

While I have killed several bears with handguns, we are talking rifle cartridges here and I see little reason to use a handgun cartridge in a rifle for hunting bears. Certainly, a .44 Rem. Mag. will do the job on a close-range bear, and I have a custom-chambered H&R single-shot in .445 Super Mag. that would be deadly, but it remains that there are far better choices in rifle cartridges. I would say the same about cartridges in the class of the .30-30 Win. That it has killed a lot of bears is undeniable, but I would not include it on a list of good bear guns.

The .243 Win. is too light, and in my experience, so is the 7mm-08 Rem. In theory, these calibers should make decent bear guns, but the bears I have seen shot with them have left me less than impressed. The .260 Rem. is in the same class. The

.308 Win. can do the job, but it's still a shadow of a .30-06 if they are loaded to equal pressures.

Long-action cartridges, starting with the .270 Win., using quality 150-grain bullets, are decent bear guns. Moving up to the .280 Rem., a 160-grain bullet does the trick, and for the .30-06, it's hard to beat the 180-grainers. If there is one truly great bear cartridge in this family, it's the .35 Whelen.

The .444 Marlin and the .45-70 Gov. are a couple of excellent short-range bear cartridges. The problem they both have is poor factory-loaded ammo available from the big three manufacturers. The .444 Marlin is available only in a 240-grain bullet designed for handguns. The "triple-four" is a better bear gun when it's loaded with a 250-grain Nosler Partition-HG or a 300-grain Swift A-Frame bullet. The .45-70 Gov. is loaded to mild pressures because the lawyers are afraid that all the old Springfield rifles will blow up if idiots put ammo in them that they shouldn't. This may be a justifiable fear. In a modern gun, though, a good handload, or one

These rifles represent opposite ends of the bear gun spectrum, but in the right situations both are excellent black bear rifles. Pictured at left is a Ruger M-77 in .300 Winchester with Nikon scope and at right is a Marlin 1895SS in .45-70 Government with Weaver scope.

Lessons about Bear Guns

My Uncle Butch learned a lesson about bear guns 35 years ago when he shot a big bear while deer hunting from our family deer camp. He was using an old Marlin lever action in .38-55, and his first shot hit the bear a little too far back and struck the liver. The question has been raised many times as to whether the bear charged, or if in his confusion chose that direction to run, but he let out a roar and came right at Butch. When the last bullet in the gun hit the bear in the head, Butch had to jump out of the way to avoid being run over as it skidded past.

The odd thing is that Butch usually loaded the tube magazine, worked the action to chamber a shell and went hunting. But for some reason, that morning he had put another shell in the magazine to replace the one that he chambered. That was the shot that killed the bear.

Butch bought a .270 Win. the next week.

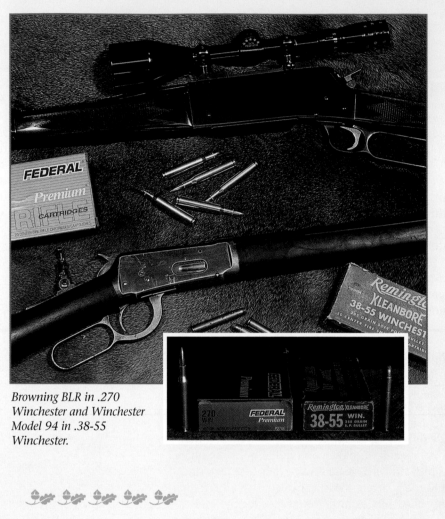

Browning BLR in .270 Winchester and Winchester Model 94 in .38-55 Winchester.

of the semi-custom loads on the market, makes the .45-70 Gov. a bad-dude bear gun. My favorite handload uses a Speer 400-grain flat-nosed bullet at almost 1,800 fps.

Any belted magnum, .270 or larger, will be bad news for bears. The best include the 7mms, Remington or Weatherby, with 160- to 175-grain bullets and any of the .300 magnums with 180- or 200-grain bullets. The .338 Win. Mag. and .340 Wthby Mag. shine with 225- or 250-grain bullets. Some hunters will argue that these are more gun than is really needed, but on the other hand, they are great insurance. That might also be said about the .375 H&H Mag.; it's more gun

than needed, but rest assured, you can't kill a bear too dead.

Years ago, I helped track a bear that was hit with a .375 H&H Mag. with a 270-grain bullet. Not too far down the blood trail, we found a chunk of his liver that we later took back to camp and put on a scale; it weighed a quarter pound. The bear was lying quite dead not far beyond.

That's my kind of bear gun.

ELK GUNS

When it comes to hunting, elk have been my cross to bear. I have never been a lucky hunter, and every critter of any description I have taken has been at a premium price paid in the currency of sweat, tears and often a little blood. Yet with perseverance I have managed to find success with most, and if not on the first attempt, certainly soon after.

Except elk.

My first elk hunt was in Montana more years ago than I care to admit. Severe weather had driven the elk off the mountains and into the "no-hunting-allowed" winter range, leaving us to wander in the now-empty mountains.

Four years later I was again in Montana. We packed deep into the mountains near Glacier National Park, and for 10 cold November days we didn't see our camp during daylight. Each day was spent looking hard for elk, but in the end nobody had even seen one.

Then came the hunt from hell.

I booked for a September bugle season hunt in southern British Columbia with what turned out to be a psychotic outfitter. In two days we hunted less than four hours while she slid further into irrationality. Her bizarre behavior led to a nasty confrontation, so I decided to leave camp. I learned

later from others that it got worse.

In the dark and lonely hours of the nights spent in a hotel waiting for a plane out of there, I thought that perhaps I should accept that I was not destined to be an elk hunter.

Still, elk haunted me. I love the mountains where they dwell, and the process of elk hunting is as engaging as any hunting I have experienced. Unable to resist the mountains' calling, the next fall found me in a Wyoming camp near the border of Yellowstone Park.

This time, before we really even got started, we were into elk, and only a few hours after the start of the hunt we were looking at a good 6x6 bull hiding in the burned timber on the next ridge. It was a long shot at a little piece of elk neck, but I hadn't endured all that pain and come this far to take any chances with my equipment. If I failed to take an elk, I'd be damned if it was going to be because of something so easily controlled as my gun.

Before I even recovered from the recoil, the guide was slapping my back and yelling something about a great shot. The elk dropped so fast that I missed seeing it, and I refused to allow myself any elation until I had my hands on his rack.

We found him lying on the tracks he had been stand-

Elk have always haunted me. I love the mountains where they dwell and the process of elk hunting is as engaging as any hunting I have experienced.

ing in. The 225-grain Barnes X-Bullet had broken—no, shattered—his neck. It was a classic case of preparation meeting opportunity. Good equipment and lots of practice paid off.

ELK ARE TOUGH

Elk hunting has changed since Jack O'Connor, Warren Page and Les Bowman roamed those Wyoming mountains. Today's opportunities on good bulls are harder to find, and many of the best elk are taken in the thick timber at far shorter ranges. Shot placement angles are not always as controllable, and hunters in the know choose a big caliber with heavy, premium bullets that will penetrate from any angle.

A big bull elk weighs 600 to 800 pounds or more—they are the tough guys of the deer family. They will take hits that would put the much-larger moose down for good, yet an elk might run to the other side of the mountain. Bull elk are notorious for their determination and tenacity, and if you don't kill them well, they can lead you on a chase you will regret to your last breath.

They have thick hides that are often caked with mud; behind that are big, tough muscles and massive bones. A big bull can soak up a lot of bullet energy, and "too much gun" is a lot better than "not enough." To cause enough damage to something as big as an elk, you need deep penetration to reach important organs.

DON'T UNDER-GUN YOURSELF

So what makes an elk gun? Most articles on elk rifles deal with cartridges that are adequate, and certainly a lot of cartridges can get the job done under most conditions. For a resident hunter who not only lives with the elk but has plenty of opportunity to hunt and is probably looking for meat as much as anything else, these adequate rifles might make sense. But we are addressing rifles for the hunter who has

Elk are big, tough, hard to kill ... and live in places where there are hell-holes you don't want them running to. Bottom line? Use enough gun to hit them hard and drop them quickly.

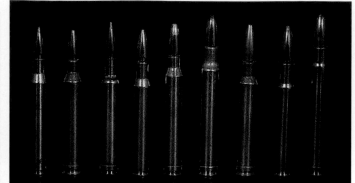

All these cartridges will take elk, but the best cartridges start at .30 caliber. Pictured (left to right): .280 Rem., 7mm Rem. Mag., 7mm Weatherby Mag., .30-06, .300 Win. Mag., .300 Weatherby Mag., .338 Win. Mag., .35 Whelen and .375 H&H.

saved for years and may not be able to hunt elk again for a while. This hunter has only the few days of vacation to hunt, and the ultimate goal is a trophy bull. The hunter cannot pick and choose the shots; the first ethical opportunity must be taken no matter what it presents. This raises the demands on rifle and cartridge selection.

Although cross-canyon and other long shots are not uncommon, it's just as likely that a hunter will need to shoot at a patch of elk hide showing through 50 yards of brush. Shot angles are not always the best, and if the hunter waits for a better chance, often the bull will melt into the brush and disappear. Most serious elk hunters today are using big, powerful cartridges with heavy, premium-quality bullets. They want a bullet that will penetrate to an elk's vitals from any angle and anchor the bull. They also want a rifle that is relatively light and easy to carry while hunting in the rough, high country that is commonly associated with elk hunting.

Currently, there are no short-action calibers fitting those criteria. The .308 Win. and 7mm-08 Rem. can kill elk, but they fall short of our definition of an elk gun. Risking the wrath of the O'Connor fan club, I will also eliminate the .270 Win. and anything smaller. The heaviest bullet you can get in a .270 Win. factory load is 150 grains, and that's not enough. The .280 Rem. might work with 160-grain bullets, but I'll not include it on my list of serious elk guns.

GETTING INTO THE RIGHT CALIBERS

Real elk guns start with the .30-06 Springfield, and then only with the best premium-quality 180-grain bullets. Even at that, you will need to pick your shots. A rear-on quartering angle requiring lots of penetration to reach the chest cavity is not favorable to a .30-06.

The .35 Whelen is excellent—particularly if you use the heavy 225- to 250-grain bullets necessary for good penetration—but is a bit limited for long-range shooting.

The 7mm Rem. Mag. was developed and tested on elk. It and the nearly identical 7mm Wthby Mag. are viable elk

The most popular rifle for elk hunting is a bolt action, and most hunters today prefer a light, synthetic-stock rifle chambered for a powerful cartridge. Pictured at left: Browning Synthetic Stalker in .300 Winchester Magnum; and at right: Winchester Model 70 WinLight in .338 Winchester Magnum. The .300 Winchester Magnum and .338 Winchester Magnum are excellent cartridges for hunting elk.

A Great Elk Gun

A big bull elk may be one of hardest-won trophies in North America. Don't risk blowing it due to something as controllable as the gun you will use.

On that long-ago hunt in Wyoming mentioned in the lead-in to this section, I used a Winchester WinLight Model 70 in .338 Win. Mag. topped with a Leupold 2.5-8X Vari-X III scope. This synthetic-stock rifle weighs only eight pounds and is a great rig for elk. (I was just happy that after lugging it for so many miles and years, I finally got to shoot it at one.) My handload consisted of a Barnes 225-grain X-Bullet pushed to 2,800 fps by 75 grains of RL-19 powder. It is one of the most accurate loads I tested in this gun, and it certainly worked on that bull.

Because this gun is no longer made, if I wanted a new elk rig I would look at any other lightweight bolt action in .338 Win. Mag. If I could afford it, I would likely pick the Remington Custom Shop Custom KS Mountain Rifle, or the Remington Alaskan Wilderness Rifle. If I had a few more dollars to spend, I would call Mark Bansner and have him build one of his Ultimate Rifles in .338 Win. Mag. for me.

If money were tight (and when is it not?), the Remington 700 SS is made in .338 Win. Mag. I just wish Remington would return to a bolt-locking safety.

guns but are at their best when loaded with high-quality 175-grain bullets. The trouble is, most hunters want the high velocity of lighter bullets, so they hunt with guns and ammo designed for shooting deer. The 7mm STW adds a bit more velocity and energy to the bullet, and with the new Winchester 160-grain Fail Safe load, it finally has a decent bullet for true big game like elk.

Any of the .300 magnums need 200-grain bullets to fill their potential. The 180-grains sometimes fail to get all the way through, and I am from the school that believes that all bullets should exit the animal. Bigger cases simply mean more velocity and more energy. The .300 Wthby Mag. tops the .300 Win. Mag., and the .300 Rem. Ultra Mag. beats them both. The .30-378 Wthby Mag. is the king of the .30 calibers.

The .340 and .338-378 Wthby Mag. are very powerful cartridges that will work quite well for elk, but many hunters cannot handle the fierce recoil, even with the heavy rifles in which the cartridges are chambered. If you can shoot them and you don't mind lugging a big rifle, they merit consideration.

If chambered in a rifle that is light enough to allow practical use in the elk mountains, the .375 H&H Mag. is an outstanding elk cartridge. Using bullets of 270 to 300 grains, it shoots relatively flat, and it certainly packs a lot of punch. Some hunters will argue that it's too big, but at the risk of redundancy, better too big than too small. The problem is that most .375 H&H rifles are too heavy. There are exceptions if you seek them out, particularly in the custom rifle route.

Arguably the best elk cartridge today is the .338 Win. Mag. When using high-quality bullets of 225 to 250 grains, it shoots flat enough for the long shots and packs enough energy and momentum to penetrate elk with an expanded bullet from any angle. It sure did the job for me in Wyoming.

Did breaking the ice with that Wyoming elk change my luck?

Well, sort of.

That was a long time ago, and I have been on several elk hunts since then. The bulls still come very hard, but you know what? I think that secretly, that's what I like about elk hunting.

MOOSE GUNS

The little bull had been harassing a cow for about 20 minutes, and with dark now getting ready to close the deal, the question was, would the big fella show or was this one all we would see this night? I turned to look at the other hunter, and for a moment I thought he was a kid waiting in line at Disney World; the excitement was buzzing through his face.

"You want that bull?" I asked, surprised.

It was my shot, so the guide looked at me when the other hunter answered yes, and I shrugged.

The gun roared five times as the bull ran around the small bog, clearly dazed and confused. The hunter reloaded quickly, and three more shots cut the Newfoundland stillness before mercifully the final bullet hit the bull's spine and he dropped.

"I told you this .270 was a killer," the hunter repeated again and again as he tried to burn off the adrenaline surge while the guide and I struggled to quarter the beast with flashlights held in our mouths.

The guy could shoot, I'll give him that much, and all eight shots had hit important places. But not one of the cheap 130-grain bullets had penetrated all the way through the moose, and he was a small one as far as moose go. Most of the bullets didn't even make the off-side hide and had stopped somewhere in the chest cavity. You might argue that the dead moose was proof enough that the .270 Win. is a moose gun, but don't try it with me.

Contrast that with the big old bull that we found high in the mountains of northern British Columbia the year before. This bull was big bodied, and even at more than 250 yards, he looked huge. I settled into a solid rest across my backpack, and when it looked right, I squeezed the trigger. By the time I had worked the bolt for a follow-up shot, the moose was lying on his back with his feet in the air. That reaction prompted our stoic guide to utter the only complete sentence I heard in the 10 days we spent with him, "Dat t'ree-seven-five one damn sure fine good moose gun!"

He was right on the assessment, if not the pronunciation. The .375 H&H Mag. with a 300-grain Nosler Partition bullet was more than up for the job. Some hunters might argue that it's really too much gun for moose, but not with me or that guide. This time the dead moose proved it well.

BIG CUSTOMER, BIG GUN

Moose are the largest land mammal in North America. Depending on where you are hunting them, a big bull will usually weigh more than 1,000 pounds. A good Alaska or Yukon bull might approach a ton. They have thick hides, tough, bulky muscles, and massive bones. They not only require a lot of penetration, but it takes a good amount of bullet weight and energy to put them down. Lightweight or poorly constructed bullets can fail miserably and never make

Moose are big. A so-so bull might weigh "only" 1,000 pounds, a big one in the North 1,400 or 1,500 pounds. Even an adult Shiras moose will weigh 900 to 1,200 pounds. Don't expect that your deer rifle will be enough gun!

it into the moose far enough to mess up the important stuff.

So what's a good, rather than just adequate, moose gun? Sure, there are a lot of cartridges that can take moose, but here we are considering those cartridges that are not just able to do the job but are well suited to do it without compromise. We are talking about guns to hunt big, trophy bull moose where controlling the variables may be tough. These are guns that can be relied on to take the shot and penetrate to the vitals on even the biggest and best from the worst angles. We are talking here about guns that are truly "damn sure fine good moose guns."

Currently, there are no short-action calibers that are worthy of the title of moose gun. The .358 Win. might have qualified, but barely, and just try to find a rifle chambered for it in a recent catalog. The .308 Win. and 7mm-08 Rem. are fine deer guns, but moose are 10 or 12 times bigger than the average whitetail; these runts don't measure up here.

I will also eliminate the .270 Win. and any cartridge with a smaller bullet diameter, even with the current crop of better bullets. The .280 Rem. might work with 175-grain bullets, but since no factory load uses them, it's off the list.

GETTING INTO STUFF THAT CAN DO THE JOB

Reluctantly, I'll start the real moose gun list with the .30-06 Springfield. But use only the very best premium quality 180-grain bullets and a careful shot selection.

I know firsthand that the .35 Whelen is an excellent moose thumper. I shot a moose during Vermont's second modern moose season in 1994 with a .35 Whelen and handloaded 225-grain Barnes X-Bullet. It broke both shoulders, exited and broke his jaw. The moose ran all of 10 feet before dropping.

The Federal Premium with the 225-grain Trophy Bonded bullet is the best .35 Whelen factory load choice. The only other factory load to consider is the Remington 250-grain; avoid their 200-grain loading at all costs. The lighter bullet is too soft for this cartridge, and while it works on whitetails, it will not reliably penetrate moose.

The 7mm magnums, Remington or Weatherby, are the minimum, and again with good, high-quality 175-grain bullets. The 7mm STW adds a bit more velocity and energy to the bullet. Right now the only factory load I would consider is the Winchester 160-grain Fail Safe.

The .300 Wthby Mag., .300 Rem. Ultra Mag. and .30-378 Weatherby Mag. are all excellent moose guns, but they really need 200-grain bullets. I fired three shots at two different moose using a .300 Win. Mag. with 180-grain Nosler Partition bullets, and none of them exited. I am from the school that believes that all bullets should exit the animal, and the next time I take any .300 magnum moose hunting, it will be loaded with 200-grain premium-quality bullets.

If there is one perfect moose cartridge, it is likely the .338 Win. Mag. When loaded with a quality 225- or 250-grain bullet, it is as if you sat down and designed it for moose hunting.

This Newfoundland moose was taken with a .30-06. The hunter and guide had called to the bull for several hours, and when the bull finally came into sight, the hunter thought to himself, "This gun isn't big enough to kill something like that!"

As that British Columbian guide noted, the .375 H&H Mag. is an excellent moose cartridge. The Federal 300-grain Nosler Partition or Trophy Bonded loads are among the best factory fodder, as are either of the two X-Bullet loads from PMC or the Speer Nitrex load with a 285-grain Grand Slam bullet. But my money goes with the Winchester 270-grain Fail Safe. The heavier 300-grain Fail Safe will work but is probably more bullet than you need and doesn't shoot as flat.

Obviously, any of the .416 or larger cartridges will smack a bull more than hard enough, but they really are more gun than you need, and most I have used are too damn heavy.

Finally, let's not forget the old .45-70 Gov. If you are hunting in the thick stuff where the shot will be close, it is something out of Bullwinkle's darkest nightmares. Forget using factory loads—they're a poor choice for moose hunting. The lawyers won't allow loading them hot enough, and you have to either handload or use ammo from a custom loader.

Just remember that when you are hunting moose, pull that trigger hard, "'cuz they're real big!"

Factory .45-70 loads are loaded to mild pressures. The .45-70 is a much better moose gun if you use handloads or custom loads.

Cartridge & Bullet	Muzzle	100-yd	200-yd	300-yd
	Velocity (in fps)	Velocity (in fps)	Velocity (in fps)	Velocity (in fps)
	Energy (in fp)	Energy (in fp)	Energy (in fp)	Energy (in fp)
	Momentum (in fp)	Momentum (in fp)	Momentum (in fp)	Momentum (in fp)
7mm Rem. Mag. Speer Nitrex 175-gr. Grand Slam	2,850 fps 3,157 fp 71.25 fp	2,652 fps 2,734 fp 66.31 fp	2,463 fps 2,358 fp 61.58 fp	2,282 fps 2,023 fp 57.04 fp
.30-06 Springfield 180-gr. Winchester Fail Safe	2,700 fps 2,914 fp 69.43 fp	2,485 fps 2,468 fp 63.89 fp	2,279 fps 2,077 fp 58.62 fp	2,084 fps 1,736 fp 53.59 fp
.300 Win. Mag. Remington Safari 200-gr. Swift A-Frame	2,825 fps 3,545 fp 80.71 fp	2,594 fps 2,990 fp 74.13 fp	2,375 fps 2,506 fp 67.86 fp	2,167 fps 2,085 fp 61.91 fp
.35 Whelen Federal 225-gr. Trophy Bonded	2,600 fps 3,378 fp 83.57 fp	2,400 fps 2,879 fp 77.15 fp	2,209 fps 2,440 fp 71.02 fp	2,027 fps 2,054 fp 65.16 fp
.338 Win. Mag. Winchester 230-gr. Fail Safe	2,780 fps 3,948 fp 91.34 fp	2,572 fps 3,380 fp 84.52 fp	2,374 fps 2,878 fp 71.99 fp	2,184 fps 2,437 fp 71.76 fp
.375 H&H Mag. Winchester 270-gr. Fail Safe	2,670 fps 4,275 fp 102.99 fp	2,449 fps 3,596 fp 94.45 fp	2,238 fps 3,004 fp 86.33 fp	2,038 fps 2,491 fp 78.61 fp

Elk & Moose Guns

GUNS FOR SHEEP & GOATS

I must confess, I have never shot a sheep. But I have been where they live and close enough to shoot them. All I lacked, depending on where I was at the time, was either a hard-to-draw permit or a big enough bank account. I will keep striving for both and fully expect to hunt them soon.

When I do, you can bet I'll give serious thought to my rifle selection. Because I have been in sheep country, the number one thing I will look at will be weight. It is steep and rocky where most sheep live. It's steep and rocky where I live too; the difference is I am at 800 feet above sea level, while most sheep can add at least another zero to the elevation of their residence. The air up there is stingy with its oxygen, and the lighter the rifle I'll have to carry, the happier my legs and lungs will be.

The rifle must also be accurate; that's a given. If it won't shoot all its bullets into less than one M.O.A., it will not be considered.

Now for the cartridge. The list starts with the .270 Win., mostly for reasons of tradition. When hunters of my generation (40-something) speak of sheep hunting, we inevitably think of Jack O'Connor and his beloved .270 Win. Any list of sheep hunting guns that omits it would border on sacrilege. Any other cartridge from the .280 through the .300 Mag. would be appropriate, providing it's in a rifle light enough to lug.

While there are, of course, many factory rifles that will meet a sheep hunter's needs, most hunters who can afford

sheep hunting have the resources to consider a custom rifle. If you were even inclined to buying a custom or semi-custom rifle, sheep hunting may be the catalyst you need. It's here that you can find the lightweight, powerful cartridges and supreme accuracy that this demanding hunting will require.

I am currently waiting delivery on a rifle from Mark Bansner that will make the ideal sheep gun. It's based on a Remington Model Seven action with a new barrel chambered for a short-action .300 cartridge that matches the ballistics of the .300 Win. Stocked with one of Mark's custom synthetic handles, it will weigh about six pounds. It will wear a Leupold 2.5-8 Vari-X III scope in David Gentry Feather-Light Rings & Bases.

All I'll lack then is the sheep tag.

I have never shot a goat either. The only one I have seen while hunting was in a place I would rather not go to without a helicopter. It seems that goats live in even more rugged country than sheep do, and I've heard they're tough customers. I would stay with the criteria for selecting a sheep gun, only looking for the lightest, most powerful rifle I could find. That and a very rugged guide who could carry me up the mountains on his back!

Of course, I'll tip him well.

THE CASE FOR "SHORT & FAT"

*I*t was on a plane going someplace to hunt deer that I found the flyer advertising a charity run.

"The Short Fat Guy's Downhill 1.5-Mile Marathon." Elapsed times were open-ended, and if you needed fuel, there was a doughnut stand at the halfway point.

If I had more time, I would have entered. I could have been a contender.

I say it's about time we got some respect. We "dimensionally challenged" folks have been discriminated against in modern society for far too long.

Back off, you beanpoles, our time has come!

The recent prejudices in deer calibers have some striking parallels. The solid calibers of Gramp's generation have fallen from grace and are now considered second-class in favor of the long, sleek numbers of today.

Long, thin bottlenecked cartridges with tiny anorexic bullets govern, while the even sleeker magnums rule.

This tyranny will not stand!

We demand a voice. Short-fat calibers have rights too and will not be ignored. Their true image is one of solid, conservative power. A short and fat (S-F) gets the job done without flash or sizzle, but with dependability, muscle and bull-headed determination. If, like most of us, you shoot your deer in the thick stuff and the distances are relatively close, then you owe it to society and to yourself to give an S-F cartridge a try.

The short and stocky calibers of Gramp's generation have fallen from grace and are now considered second class in favor of today's long and sleek cartridges.

You Can't "Overkill" Them

*A*s my deer hunting experience expands to include more animals with more cartridges, I am becoming convinced that bullet size does indeed matter.

I have come to believe that it's a good idea to hit animals with something big, particularly when you are hunting mature trophy animals. I like bigger-diameter bullets, but just as important, plenty of bullet weight and enough velocity. Given a choice, I will pick a long-action cartridge and use a bullet that is slightly on the heavy side for the cartridge. For example, when deer hunting, I truly like the .30-06 with a quality 165-grain bullet or the .280 Rem. with a 150- or 160-grain bullet. Better still, a 7mm Mag., Remington or Weatherby, with a 160-grain bullet, or a .300 Mag., Winchester or Weatherby, with 180-grain bullets. The reason is that you really can't "overkill" a deer, but you can surely "underkill" him.

Coincidentally, I was hunting coyotes in Texas last year with Winchester's Mike Jordan, who has been at it a long time and knows his stuff when it comes to shooting. After I voiced this opinion, he told me that after years of talking with those gun and hunting writers who have a lot of experience shooting big game, the universal theme from them is exactly that. Just as Robert Ruark said posthumously, "Use enough gun." Sure, an *adequate* cartridge will handle 99 percent of the game you shoot, but sooner or later it will let you down. With a bigger cartridge, the margin for error is greater, and while they too can fail, the odds against it are far better than with the lighter cartridges.

This principle applies to any big game animal you might be hunting. You can never go wrong by selecting a cartridge and bullet that are considered on the big side of those suitable for the job.

S-F Calibers

It may be a bit cliché in gun writing, but the .44 Rem. Mag. is one of those calibers whose performance on game seems out of proportion with its paper ballistics. In a carbine such as Marlin's Model 1894, it spits a 240-grain hollow point out at 1,800 fps. I have witnessed a lot of whitetails being hit with this setup, and they all reacted favorably to the hunter's position.

The .35 Rem. has been with us since 1906, and the number of venison dinners it has accounted for would feed many a family for a good long time. Using a 200-grain bullet moving at 2,000 fps, it isn't flashy, but a deer hit stays hit.

The .356 Win. and .358 Win. are somewhat newer on the scene; the former crashed the party in 1982, but the .358 has been with us since 1955. Both push a 200-grain bullet to about 2,400 fps. Neither is currently chambered in a factory

(Left) Pictured (left to right): .30-30 Winchester, .30-06 Springfield and .30-378 Weatherby. (Right) Are Magnums necessary? If all these cartridges will take big game, why do we need magnums? Because they usually do it better, bigger and faster, that's why. It's the American way! Pictured (left to right): 7mm Weatherby Magnum, 7mm Remington Magnum, .280 Remington, .284 Winchester, 7X57 Mauser, 7mm-08 Remington and 7X30 Waters.

Magnums Have Their Place

*I*t's common to hear something like this in deer camp: "Magnums are too heavy, too expensive, too loud and kick so hard that nobody can ever shoot them well. Heck, it's a well-known fact that more deer have been killed with the old .30-30 than with any other rifle caliber, and that's no more a magnum than Snoop Doggy Dog is a country music star."

The speaker definitely has an opinion and may have a point—magnums are not for everybody. They kick like a Ninja and bellow like a castrated bull, making them difficult to shoot well. But that doesn't justify dismissing their use by those who can handle them well. Performance has a price.

If, like most of us, your brain goes into reverse when a huge buck appears, then a little margin of "screw-up room" can be comforting.

With 165-grain bullets and a 6-inch zone, a .308 Win. has a point-blank range of 257 yards; the .30-06

Springfield, 276 yards; and the .300 Wthby Mag., 321 yards, for a gain of 64 yards over the .308 Win.

The other big advantage is in retained energy. At 400 yards, the .308 Win. has dropped to 1,256 foot-pounds. That puts it in the class with the .30-30 Win. at 100 yards—and how many serious trophy hunters will use the .30-30 when they know the shots will be longer than 100 yards? At 400 yards, the .300 Wthby Mag. retains as much energy as the .308 had at 84 yards. At 320 yards, the .300 Wthby Mag. has as much remaining energy as the .308 had at the muzzle.

Remember, there are not degrees of dead. However, a deer can be wounded in degrees; all of them are bad. When trophy hunting—any hunting for that matter—it's better to err on the side of too much power.

For close-range shooting when a lot of stopping power is needed, the .444 Marlin (right) and .45-70 (left) are cartridges that will get the job done.

rifle, and that's a further indication of the discrimination that S-F calibers are subjected to. However, after hunting several seasons with both, I have come to think of them as among the best woods calibers for deer. My .356 is a Winchester Model 94 lever action mounted with a low power scope. It is quite accurate; I love the way it feels in my hand and how it handles in the woods. When polled, deer, on the other hand, claim to hate it.

The great gun writer Colonel Whelen's name is carried on in the .35 Whelen. I am not sure if it qualifies as an S-F caliber because it's a little too tall. But I'll include it anyway just because it isn't getting the respect it deserves, simply because of prejudices against its corpulent bullet diameter.

The Whelen will push a 200-grain bullet to 2,600 fps. I believe I have tried all the rifles regularly chambered for this caliber, but my favorite is a Remington 7600 pump action. When it is in my hands, I feel confident. You might ask the deer involved how that confidence translates into shooting,

but most of them have been digested; the rest are chilling out in the freezer.

THE *BIG* GUYS

Then there are the big brothers, the ones who scare off the bullies, the ones that the little fellas look up to: the .45-70 Gov. and the .444 Marlin.

The .45-70 Gov. started life as a military caliber, and like most that are good, it has survived. In a Marlin lever action or a modern single-shot, it's a good deer caliber with factory loads. But those loads are loaded to anemic velocities because of all the old Springfield rifles around that can't handle much pressure. While they will take deer without trouble, I have to agree with the Army that you should "be all you can be!" To achieve the full potential of the .45-70 Gov., you must handload. My favorite handload for my Marlin shoots .400 Remington Speer bullets at 1,800 fps. It's very accurate, and I understand that the deer have a petition circulating calling for a government ban!

Marlin's proprietary .444 is an elongated .44 Rem. Mag. Remington's factory loads shoot a 240-grain bullet at 2,350 fps. Bucks hit with this load have a bleak future indeed.

Let's stop perpetuating this discrimination and give equal rights to all deer calibers, not just those sleek enough to be "politically correct."

Long live the "stubby" motif!

Big Stuff

Bullet energy tables are heavily biased to velocity, but a light, superfast bullet is not the way to go with big critters. Sure, they show lots of energy, but energy doesn't kill game—tissue damage does that. To cause enough damage to something big (more than 500 pounds), you need deep penetration to reach the stuff that needs damaging. For several reasons, light, fast bullets do not penetrate well.

In addition to energy, a cartridge for true big game should be chosen on momentum, which places equal importance on bullet weight and velocity. The absolute minimum momentum that should be considered for hunting the big stuff that can't eat you is 55 lbs-fps at impact, not at the muzzle. This means a bullet of at least 180 grains with an impact velocity of at least 2,100 fps.

The bullet must also be built so that it will maintain

its weight well enough to carry the momentum and energy while continuing to penetrate. If a bullet breaks up and loses weight, it not only loses energy and momentum from the loss of retained weight, but loses the energy used to tear the bullet apart as well. A well-designed bullet will use only the minimum energy needed to expand to an optimum frontal area and then controls that expansion and uses its remaining energy to facilitate penetration.

When hunting things that bite, primarily the big bears here in North America, I would look for momentum of 80 lbs-fps on impact. That's a 250-grain bullet with an impact velocity of 2,240 fps. You might consider something less, but personally, I don't intend to make it a fair fight.

Chapter 3

BULLETS

*I*f the biggest expert in the field gave an outdoor show seminar on today's rifle bullets, there likely wouldn't be much need for crowd control.

That's a little troubling because your bullet is your one physical connection with the game, the sole determiner of the outcome of any hunt because you touch a live animal with nothing else. Yet the rifle bullet remains the wallflower of the dance, sitting in a corner while everybody is caught up with the glamour and paying it no attention.

The bottom line is that everything you do on any hunt—all the expense, the time, the sweat and the tears—all comes down to one thing: the bullet. If the bullet does its job, you are happy and it's forgotten. If it does not, you have nobody but yourself to blame.

The bullet is truly the unsung hero of the modern big-game rifle hunter. The demands placed on it are incredible. We expect our bullets to work correctly over a range of impact velocity and target variations that would be deemed unreasonable by any objective outside observer. And the bullets do it so well that we virtually ignore that these physical principles exist.

But to think today's advances have taken bullet design as far as it can possibly go would be fool's thinking. There is always one more hill to climb, one more frontier to conquer and one more problem to solve. As long as we are free to own and shoot rifles and as long as those rifles continue to use bullets as projectiles, we will continue to witness both subtle and amazing technological advances in bullet design.

And we as hunters will continue to virtually ignore the bullets we shoot, demanding perfection and expecting and receiving nothing less.

MATCHING THE BULLET TO THE GAME

odern hunting ammo's ancestry can be traced to the first self-contained metallic cartridge, the .22 Short, introduced by S&W in 1857. By the mid-1860s, metallic cartridges were off and running, and with the introduction of smokeless powder in 1885, we entered the "small bore-high velocity" era.

With the move to smaller, faster bullets, it was discovered that lead bullets were too soft to hold the rifling as the slug sped down the bore. That necessitated the invention of the jacketed bullet, which of course led to even more developments.

For example, the first .30-06 bullets used a jacket alloy of 85 percent copper and 15 percent nickel. While this was fine in lesser calibers (like the .30-30), it fouled bores at .30-06 velocities. A switch was made to an alloy of 5 or 10 percent zinc to 95 or 90 percent copper. Called gilding metal, this is still in common use for jacket material in today's bullets.

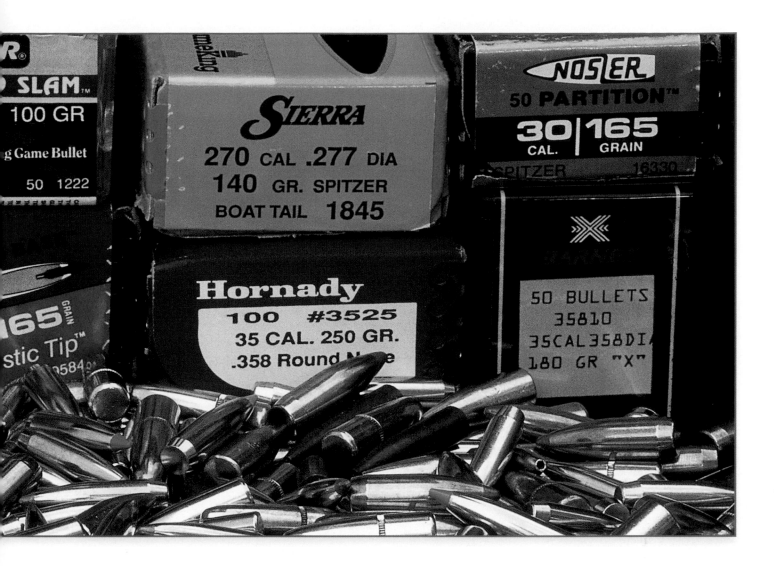

The velocities of rifles soon crept past 3,000 fps, and the problem then became how to build a bullet that would stay together at high velocity and still perform well over the entire spectrum of the extended ranges that this new speed allowed.

A bullet that expanded well at 300 yards would often tear apart with a 50-yard impact. The bullet usually killed deer-sized game instantly but accounted for the reputation that early magnum calibers had for excessive meat destruction. On bigger game, particularly game that can bite you, the results could be a disaster for all involved. Yet if the bullet was tough enough for the close-range impacts, it often failed to expand at long range and at the resulting reduced velocity, allowing wounded game to escape or often convincing less-than-observant hunters that they had missed.

LOOKING FOR THE PERFECT BULLET

Clearly the technology that created the attainable velocities was advanced beyond that of the bullets that were making the journey. For gunwise hunters in the know, the solution for years was to

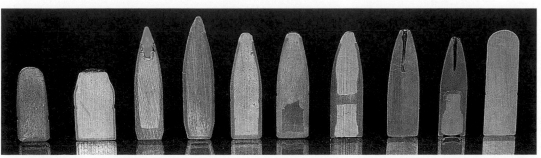

Great advances in bullet designs have allowed hunters to match the bullet to the game. It has also allowed the development of higher velocity cartridges. Bullet designs left to right: Hornady Round Nose, Speer Flat Nose, Nosler Ballistic Tip, Sierra Boat Tail, Hornady InterLock, Speer Grand Slam, Nosler Partition, Barnes X-Bullet, Winchester Fail Safe and Barnes Solid.

The sectioned bullets show the construction while the bullets recovered from game show how terminal performance differs. Pictured (left to right): Combined Technologies Fail Safe, Combined Technologies Partition Gold Rifle, Nosler Partition, Swift A-Frame, Nosler Ballistic Tip and Barnes X-Bullet.

try to match the anticipated game and range to the bullet. With the manufacturers of factory ammo, it was primarily to use a compromise bullet somewhere in the middle.

The quest was to create a bullet that would expand very early in the terminal ballistic path and within a wide impact velocity range, then control the expansion after achieving the desired frontal area and continue to penetrate while remaining intact. Some of today's bullets are getting pretty close to that goal.

Since its 1948 debut, the Nosler Partition has been the benchmark that all other big-game bullets have been judged by. This bullet has two lead cores separated by a solid "partition" of jacket material. The theory is that the front end of the bullet will expand easily and rapidly, while the rear section is protected by the partition. The bullet will not expand past this partition, so this ensures that the rear portion will remain intact to continue to drive the bullet through the target even after the front core is gone.

It's doubtful that any big game animal exists that has not been taken with the Partition bullet. From pronghorns to moose, it has always risen to the call and performed admirably. The Partition bullet will almost always continue to expand until it loses the front core and about 40 percent of its weight. The jacket will then fold back against the rear section, creating a smaller frontal area. While this results in good penetration, it also creates small exit holes that lead the uninformed to believe that the bullet didn't expand. While the technology is 50 years old and there are certainly more advanced bullets on the market today, the Partition is still a favorite for many experienced big game hunters.

The Partition is available from Nosler for handloading and in factory ammo from several companies, including Remington, Winchester and Federal. Winchester's version is an "improved" partition bullet called the Partition Gold Rifle. It moves the partition forward to increase weight retention while strengthening the rear section with a steel liner. Also, the Partition Gold bullet is molybdenum (moly) coated.

MAKING AN EVEN BETTER BULLET

The Swift A-Frame bullet builds on the Nosler Partition design. It also uses a partition of metal separating two distinct

cores of lead alloy, but with some design differences. The most dominant difference is that the front core is bonded to the tapered jacket to keep the two from separating while expanding, which helps in weight retention and penetration. This bullet usually has a large expanded frontal area. Remington loads the Swift A-Frame in their Safari line of factory ammo.

The Barnes X-Bullet is a real innovation in new bullet technology. It's a unique solid copper bullet with no lead core to separate from the jacket. It features a small-diameter, deep hollow point in the nose that will split into four distinct petals that expand until reaching the bottom of the hollow point. This leaves a long, solid rear section to continue to drive the expanded bullet through the target for outstanding performance. The petals "cut" through tissue as the bullet twists and penetrates. Deep, reliable penetration is the trademark of this bullet.

Recently, Barnes offered the X-Bullet with a lubricating coating called XLC, which increases velocity potential as well as reduces bore fouling. PMC and Weatherby currently load the X-Bullet in factory ammo, while Federal offers ammo with XLC-coated X-Bullets.

Perhaps the most advanced design offered today is the Winchester Fail Safe Supreme bullet. The front "half" of the bullet is solid copper alloy with a small, deep, hollow point, similar to the X-Bullet. The rear section has a lead core

Today's super bullets all act differently on impact. The smart hunter tailors his bullet performance to the game he is hunting. These .30-06 180 gr. loads were tested in water soaked newspapers for penetration, expansion and weight retention. Left to right: PMC with Barnes X-Bullet, Remington Safari with Swift A-Frame bullets, Federal Premium with Nosler Partition, and Winchester Fail Safe Supreme.

enclosed by a steel sheath and covered in a jacket formed from the same metal used for the front. The two are separated by a thick belt of solid copper alloy. Finally, the bullet is moly coated.

The Fail Safe bullet is designed to expand very quickly until it reaches the solid belt at the end of the hollow point, then stop expanding. The long rear section behind the bullet contains more weight than the front because of the denser lead and provides weight to push the bullet through the target, increasing penetration. The bullet is more conventional in its length-to-weight ratio and eliminates some of the theoretical problems of the X-Bullet, such as increased bore friction (due to the longer bullet) and loss of powder capacity because of the need to seat the longer bullet deeper into the case.

The Fail Safe bullet was number one in penetration in a test I conducted of premium bullets. Yet extensive hunting experience shows that it expands well on deer-sized game. Winchester loads this bullet in factory loads as well as offers the bullet to handloaders.

The Speer Grand Slam bullet uses a dual core of soft lead in the front bonded to a much harder rear core. The jacket is tapered to control expansion, and the core is locked to the jacket by a swaged ring of material inside the jacket. The Grand Slam expands well on deer and will penetrate on bigger game as well. As with any lead core bullet, it offers a larger total expanded frontal area than copper-nose bullets. Speer offers the bullet in its Nitrex factory ammo line as well as bullets for handloading.

The Trophy Bonded Bear Claw bullet features a shallow, bonded lead core with a long, solid base behind it. Long available for reloading, this bullet is offered by Federal in factory loads as well.

FOR THE BIGGEST GAME ...

All these super-premium bullets will work for any big-game application, but for bigger game that requires deep penetration, they are in my opinion a must. At

The bullet is the one physical connection with any game we hunt. We expect it to work correctly over a range of impact velocity and target variations that would be deemed unreasonable by any objective outside observer. Yet they do it so well that we virtually ignore that they exist.

Ballistic-tip bullets are accurate, and they retain enough velocity, even at long range, to stop game in its tracks.

line from Winchester called Ballistic Silvertip.

The Ballistic Tip was first introduced by Nosler to resist tip deformation under recoil while in the rifle's magazine. It is superbly accurate and features high ballistic coefficients that are retained until target contact for excellent velocity retention and long-range accuracy. While they are still new at this time, the Hornady SST and Swift Scirocco Polymer-Tipped bullets should deliver similar performance. Another bullet with similar terminal performance is the Sierra Game King, which also enjoys a reputation for outstanding accuracy.

Somewhere in between are bullets like the Hornady InterLock, Remington Core-Lokt and the Speer Hot Core. These are great game bullets that deliver excellent performance for a reasonable price.

The truth be known, it's hard to find a truly poor bullet today, and now, as hunters are becoming more refined in their demands, the market will start to fill out into specific niches with bullets designed for a narrowly defined hunting situation.

REVISITING VELOCITY

Now that the bullet technology has started to catch up to the cartridges, the pendulum is swinging back to the velocity race. Just in the past few years, Weatherby has introduced a factory version of the popular wildcat .30-378 that pushes a 180-grain bullet to 3,450 fps, and a .338-378 with a muzzle velocity (MV) of 3,350 fps with a 200-grain bullet. Meanwhile, Remington is chambering the hot new factory version of the 7mm STW that cruises a 140-grain at 3,325 fps, and the new Rem. .300 Ultra Mag. launches a 180-grain Nosler Partition bullet to 3,300 fps. Expect the trend to continue as Remington builds on its Ultra Mag. family.

Hunters have never had it so good, and this trend in bullet design as well as faster cartridges to drive them will only continue, at least until somebody introduces a ray gun for hunters.

the same time, I have taken whitetails and similar-sized game with all the bullets listed above, and they have performed well across the spectrum. I prefer them for most of my hunting, but some hunters will argue that they are not really necessary for any but the largest deer, that other less-expensive bullets will work as well or better. If you subscribe to the theory of deep penetration with an expanded bullet, then there is little reason not to use these bullets. However, a large segment of the population, primarily deer hunters, wants more violent expansion. They believe in rapid expansion and even disintegration of the bullet inside the animal. The argument is that it creates more hydrostatic shock and that the disintegrating bullet sends off secondary projectiles of bullet fragments, which create even more tissue loss.

Simply to lump all hunting together would be folly. Certainly, a 150-pound whitetail buck is not the same critter as a 700-pound bull elk. For the big guys, the "super bullets" are the way to go, and you would be well advised to shoot them from big cartridges. But for hunting average-sized deer, particularly where the ranges can be long, bullets such as the Nosler Ballistic Tip will prove outstanding at delivering rapid expansion and energy transfer. You can find them factory loaded from Federal, Remington, Weatherby and in the new

Match the Bullet to the Cartridge

*E*ven though different cartridges may take the same bullets, not all the cartridges will extract the same bullet performance. You simply can't expect a bullet to act the same way from a .308 Win. as it does from a .30-378 Wthby Mag. It may be traveling nearly 1,000 fps faster from the big gun, and that changes things radically.

A good example of this is the old Nosler Ballistic Tip bullets. For a long time, many hunters thought they were too "soft" and didn't like them for big-game hunting because they tended to come apart and not exit the animal. However, when used at the lower velocities of single-shot handguns, they performed much differently, acting like a good expansion-controlled big-game bullet and penetrating very well. (Nosler has since changed the Ballistic Tip design to "toughen" it up a little, and now many of the rifle shooters who didn't like it before are embracing the Ballistic Tip as a great, but still relatively soft, big-game bullet.)

A quality bullet can make the difference when conditions are extreme. Here, bullets were fired at reduced velocity to simulate long-range hits. These bullets expanded even at reduced velocities. Left is a Barnes X-Bullet and right is a Winchester Fail Safe.

Generally speaking and with all else being equal, the larger the capacity of the case, the heavier the bullet you should use. For example, when hunting deer, a 140-grain bullet is a good choice for the 7mm-08 Rem., but a 160-grain may be far better for the 7mm Rem. Mag. Usually, the heavier the bullet within a given diameter, the tougher it is because the manufacturers expect that the heavier bullets will be used for bigger game and from bigger cases. At magnum impact velocities, the 160-grain may perform similarly to the 140-grain at the lower 7mm-08 impact velocity.

Smaller cases simply don't have the powder capacity to utilize heavy bullets well. For example, the 200-grain is an excellent weight for the .300 magnums, but trying to use it in a .308 will result in disappointment. You simply cannot push it fast enough for good performance.

On the other hand, the 150-grain is a great bullet in the .308 Win. for deer-sized game, but many 150-grain bullets will come apart on impact from a .300 Wthby Mag., thus wasting meat and failing to penetrate.

It is always best to match the cartridge to both the game being hunted and the expected shooting distances, and then match the bullet to all three. This, of course, applies to bullet design as well as weight.

These cartridges will all shoot the same bullets. However, velocity will vary by as much as 1,000 fps, so it is unreasonable to expect the bullet to perform the same with every cartridge. Left to right: .308 Winchester, .30-06 Springfield, .300 Winchester Magnum, .300 Weatherby and .30-378 Weatherby.

IN OR OUT: THE QUESTION OF BULLET PERFORMANCE

There is an increasingly popular theory that a bullet should stay in a big game animal's body, "dumping all its energy." This subject is showing up more and more wherever hunters gather. It is being promoted by several gun writers, and unfortunately, many hunters are accepting it as gospel.

Personally, I find it irresponsible.

A .22 LR will always stay in the deer, dumping all its energy and often resulting in the termination of the deer. Does that make it a deer caliber? Of course not.

When applied with a modern rifle caliber, this theory can produce some spectacular results, but those hunters who persist in using it as a guide for choosing their bullets and cartridges are courting disaster. There are far too many variables— impact velocity, bullet path, game size, material penetrated, physiological variables in the target animal and many more—for this to ever work.

Consider that a .220 Swift with a 40-grain bullet at 4,100 fps generates 1,493 foot-pounds of energy, far more than any generally accepted 1,000 foot-pounds minimum for white-tailed deer. If you place that bullet precisely in the lungs, the deer will likely drop as if hit by lightning. Move the impact a few inches forward to the shoulder, and he will probably run off. If he is lucky, the coyotes will find him soon and end his suffering. Both shots dumped all their energy into the deer's body, so what happened?

DOING REAL DAMAGE

You must remember that death is not a result of energy transfer, but of tissue destruction. Dumping energy is useless if it does not result in damage to vital tissue. The bullet that hit the shoulder likely fragmented and failed to penetrate through anything important.

White-tailed deer are our most popular big-game animal and as a result are the basis for most hunters' experiences. The fact that whitetails are relatively easy to dispatch and that most hunters today use a rifle chambered for a cartridge that is far more powerful than necessary allows even the poorest bullets to drop the deer most of the time. But with bad bullet or cartridge choices, sooner or later one of the variables will enter into the equation, and the result will be a wounding loss. Try it with bigger game, particularly something inherently tough like elk or bears, and sooner or later it will bite you in the backside. (The bear might too!)

The other end of the equation is this: A bullet that passes completely through the animal, but, because of its design,

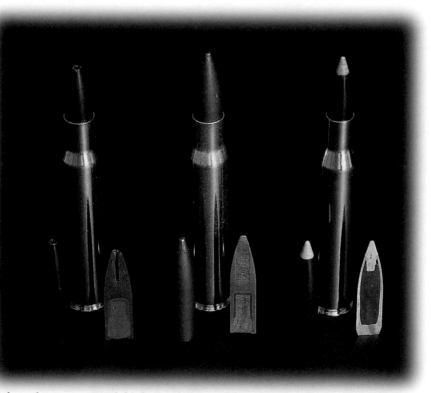

Today, a hunter can match his bullet almost exactly to the game and conditions he is hunting. Winchester has teamed up with Nosler to offer factory loads with bullets to meet any performance level. Left to right: Ballistic Silvertip, Partition Gold and Fail Safe. These bullets offer different exterior ballistics as well as greatly different terminal ballistic performance on game.

does not expand or cause adequate tissue damage, will produce results that are just as poor.

BULLETS & WOUND CHANNELS

An ethical hunter will choose a caliber of adequate power for the game hunted and match it with a quality bullet. For most North American hunting, this bullet should be designed to expand very soon after initial impact and to hold together

This trophy buck was found within sight of the stand he was shot from in North Texas. A marginal hit coupled with the bullet's failure to exit left a poor blood trail and the hunter never found the buck.

enough to continue through the animal completely, under all but the most extreme conditions.

Ideally, the bullet will retain much of its original length and weight to aid in penetration and to help keep it on its original course. This will create a substantial wound channel through every part of the animal the bullet passes through. Expansion ensures that the increased diameter of the frontal area will transfer energy to the surrounding tissue as it passes through, causing damage through actual contact, hydraulic shock and secondary projectiles such as bone fragments.

Wound channels are relative to energy transfer and the frontal area of the bullet. Consider how it would look if the animal were a homogenous material, like ballistic gelatin. As a bullet first contacts, the wound channel is bullet diameter. Then as it penetrates, the wound diameter will grow relative to the energy transferred and the contact damage caused by the expanding bullet diameter and

This New Brunswick bear weighed more than 300 pounds. He was dropped with one straight-on shot from a .308 Winchester. The keys? Plenty of power, and a good bullet that penetrated well, kept on course and created a substantial wound channel.

This relatively small-bodied Texas buck almost escaped because of poor bullet performance. With a long-range shot, the bullet did not expand properly and the buck ran off. But I watched him as he laid down several hundred yards up a hill and was able to stalk him and shoot again.

shape. If the bullet is going to stay in the game and velocity slows as energy levels drop, the wound channel diameter will again begin to taper until it reaches current bullet diameter at the point where it stops. This results in a misshapen, football-shaped wound channel, with a large maximum diameter, which is fine if it's in the right place but not if it ends short of vital tissue.

With proper bullet design and initial energy, the bullet exits with energy remaining. The resulting wound channel has a minimal decreasing profile and will remain near the maximum diameter all the way to the exit.

So what if the bullet exits with remaining energy? The important thing is that it created a sufficient wound channel completely through the target. Even though that wound channel diameter may be less at its peak than that created by a bullet that dumps all its energy and fails to exit, that wound channel is much longer and has a better chance of passing through something vital.

The results may not be as spectacular as a lung hit with a bullet that tears itself apart, dumps its energy in a short wound channel and fails to exit, but it is much more predictable, reliable and consistent. These are far more desirable traits for an ethical hunter than dramatic impact results with a high failure potential.

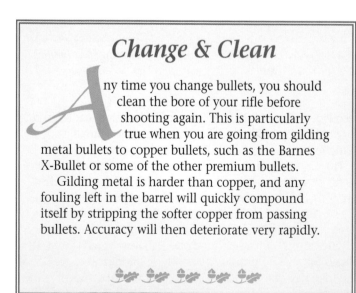

Change & Clean

Any time you change bullets, you should clean the bore of your rifle before shooting again. This is particularly true when you are going from gilding metal bullets to copper bullets, such as the Barnes X-Bullet or some of the other premium bullets.

Gilding metal is harder than copper, and any fouling left in the barrel will quickly compound itself by stripping the softer copper from passing bullets. Accuracy will then deteriorate very rapidly.

WHAT'S THE POINT?

Bullet selection is important: Gear your bullet to the game being hunted. These Nosler Ballistic Tip bullets are great for long range deer hunting with this .280 Ackley Improved. But for bear, elk or moose a tougher bullet like the Nosler Partition or Barnes X-Bullet would be better.

W hen you get down to the basics, you have three styles of bullet points to choose from: plastic-tipped, round-nosed and pointed. We'll explore plastic tips and then compare round-nosed and pointed bullets.

PLASTIC-TIPPED BULLETS

You would have to have tunnel-vision not to have noticed the trend in the last few years toward plastic-tipped bullets. Nosler started it in 1985 with its Ballistic Tip bullets, initially designed to prevent nose damage in the magazine as the rifle recoiled. Today, the Nosler Ballistic Tip bullet is loaded in factory ammo by Federal, Remington, Weatherby and Winchester.

Hornady introduced its SST (Super Shock Tipped) bullet in 1998, and it is loaded in factory ammo by Hornady. Swift introduced its own plastic-tipped big-game bullet, the Scirocco, in 1999. (Sierra's plastic-tipped bullets are currently designed only for varmint hunting.)

The primary advantage of a plastic-tipped bullet is that it allows for a sharp profile and a very small meplat (the flat leading edge of a bullet), which results in a high ballistic coefficient—the highest of any hunting bullet design, particularly when it is coupled with a boattail. Also important in a long-range bullet is the consistency of shape from bullet to bullet. The plastic nose is less likely to deform than a lead tip, and this results in a very consistent ballistic coefficient from bullet to bullet, enhancing downrange accuracy.

The lighter plastic tip also allows the center of gravity to be moved back slightly on the bullet, creating greater stability in flight while still allowing a long bearing surface. This is the same concept that allows the superior accuracy in hollow point match bullets.

ROUND-NOSED VS. POINTED BULLETS

The question of pointed vs. round-nosed bullets is one that once raised a lot of debate. There is no question that most of the development in terminal performance with today's super bullets has been in streamlined pointed styles, and right now, pointed bullets are dominating the market. Coupled with hunters' current fascination for long-range hunting, this has all but stifled the debate.

However, the round-nosed bullet still has its followers. Proponents claim that with its larger frontal area, a round nose expands more quickly and imparts more energy to the target. They likely have a point, and some deep woods hunters will hunt with nothing else.

The debate, though, has always been primarily about the external ballistics—that is, how much more quickly the round-nosed bullet loses velocity and how much more it will drop at a given range than a pointed bullet.

Let's compare Remington factory 180-grain .30-06 factory loads—one pointed, the other round nose (see graph below and table on page 73).

While there is little doubt that round-nosed bullets are deadly when

Round-nosed bullets lose velocity much faster than pointed bullets. With today's advances in bullet design there is little reason to use round-nosed bullets in rifles that can accept pointed bullets. Here are two .300 Savage loads, round-nosed on the left and pointed on right.

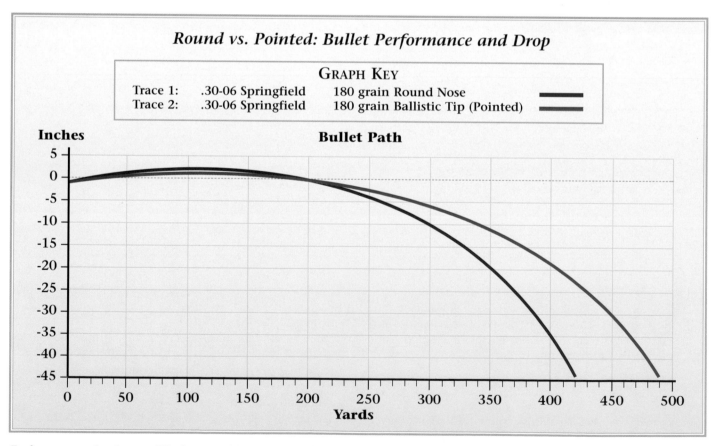

For longer-range shooting, you'll be best served by a pointed bullet, as this graph shows: A pointed bullet retains more velocity and will drop less, at a given range, than a round-nosed bullet. In fact, a pointed bullet will perform well in almost any hunting situation.

A Comparison: Pointed vs. Round-Nosed Bullets

Pointed Bullet*	Muzzle	100 Yards	200 Yards	300 Yards	400 Yards	500 Yards
Velocity (in feet per second)	2,700	2,469	2,250	2,042	1,846	1,663
Energy (in foot-pounds)	2,913	2,436	2,023	1,666	1,362	1,105
Bullet Path (in inches)	N/A	+2.1	0	-9.0	-26.3	-54.0
Round-Nosed Bullet*	**Muzzle**	**100 Yards**	**200 Yards**	**300 Yards**	**400 Yards**	**500 Yards**
Velocity (in feet per second)	2,700	2,348	2,023	1,727	1,466	1,215
Energy (in foot-pounds)	2,913	2,203	1,635	1,192	859	625
Bullet Path (in inches)	N/A	+2.4	0	-11.0	-33.8	-72.8

* Factory load, 180-grain bullet

used by hunters in the deep woods, the chart clearly shows that they shed energy much faster and drop more quickly than pointed bullets. Obviously, in guns such as lever actions with tube magazines, round-nosed or flat-nose bullets must be used, but it has by now been well established that pointed bullets kill game very well at any distance. Considering that the best of today's bullet designs, not only for external ballistics but for terminal ballistics as well, are pointed, and given a choice, there is little reason to pick a round-nosed bullet for big-game hunting.

Ballistic Coefficient & Sectional Density

Two terms that are often heard when speaking about bullets are Ballistic Coefficient (BC) and Sectional Density (SD).

Ballistic Coefficient is a measure of how aerodynamic a bullet is and how well it cuts through the air. The higher the number, the less the bullet is slowed by air resistance over a given distance at a given velocity. That means a higher BC bullet retains its velocity better than a low BC bullet, resulting in flatter trajectories and increased down-range energy retention.

There are several factors that affect the BC of a bullet, but shape is the one that is most easily identified. A pointed bullet will have a higher BC than a flat-nose or round-nose bullet of the same diameter and weight simply because it offers less wind resistance.

Sectional Density is a measure of a bullet's mass relative to its cross-section: in simple terms, a relationship of its weight to its diameter.

The higher the SD of a bullet in a given diameter, the heavier and longer that bullet will be. This is important to several factors, including the BC of the bullet. But from a big game hunter's standpoint the most relevant measure of SD is that with all else being equal, the higher the SD of a bullet the better its ability to penetrate.

Chapter 4

RIFLE CARE & MAINTENANCE

W hen you clean your rifle, you are not merely performing maintenance, you are preserving the future. Firearms, for the most part, do not participate in the marketing concept of planned obsolescence, or at least not in the sense that the gun will be worn out and useless when the newer model hits the dealer's shelves. Quality firearms are made to last, and they will be here for future generations to enjoy as we did. When you fail in caring for them, you are failing the future.

By not properly taking care of your rifle, you rob yourself of its best performance. You also rob future generations because you undoubtedly will not be the last person to own a rifle made to outlast several men. And, finally, you show a disrespect to the firearm.

As a precision machine, your rifle deserves your respect, and that's best shown with loving and knowledgeable care.

FROM THE BOX TO THE FIELD

Growing up in a small town where the primary employment was in one of a handful of manufacturing plants in the city 10 miles to the north, I was always told that you aren't supposed to enjoy work. I was brought up to believe that work was something you endured to survive; the concept of actually liking what you did all day was completely foreign.

For 20 years, I tried to be a good soldier and do as expected, working as best I could at jobs that I hated. Some paid quite well, but there had to be more to life than enduring 30 years of misery just for a pension. I tried hard, I really did, but I was miserable.

Then I discovered that I liked writing and photography and that when I did it about guns, shooting or hunting, I could even get paid. Compared to my last union job, I now work twice the hours for half the money, but I couldn't be happier!

In this business of writing about guns, I test a lot of new rifles, and I have developed a step-by-step process that I go through with any rifle that I will be hunting with. This deals primarily with bolt actions, as they are by far the most popular rifles today; however, you can easily adapt the instructions to fit any other style of rifle.

FIRST IMPRESSIONS ...

The first and most important step after opening the box is to make double sure the gun is unloaded. Next is to read all the literature enclosed, including the owner's manual, and to become completely familiar with all features of the rifle. Also, before proceeding, make sure at this point that you have all the correct ammunition, scope mounts and any other accessories for the rifle.

Any work you will be doing will likely require screwdrivers or hex wrenches, and it is imperative that they fit into the screws correctly. The sides of the screwdriver blades should have parallel edges. Most screwdrivers sold in hardware stores have tapered sides that should never be used for working on guns. Also, any screwdriver must fit exactly in the slot of the screw it is being used on. The reason for this is that a tapered or poor-fitting screwdriver will ride out of the slot as torque is applied, which is guaranteed to add some unwanted engraving to your new rifle.

Another "must-have" tool is a gun cradle to hold your rifle while you work. The first time you slip while trying to loosen a stubborn screw and stab a screwdriver through your shooting hand you will agree.

STOCK, TRIGGERS & SWIVELS

Take the stock off and, if it's wood, treat all unsealed areas with polyurethane to help control dimension changes caused by moisture. These areas include the barrel channel and all bedding areas. Don't forget to remove the butt pad and treat

Seal all exposed wood on a new rifle stock to prevent moisture that could affect the wood and cause changes.

that area. The first couple of coats should be thinned according to the instructions on the can so that they soak well into the wood. Allow one coat to dry before applying the next. End with a final coat or two of uncut polyurethane, but be cautious in critical bedding areas, such as around the recoil lug, to avoid buildup that can affect bedding. Set the stock aside to dry thoroughly.

Next, turn your attention to the trigger. If it doesn't break clean and crisp with little creep or overtravel and if it is not in the 3- to 5-pound pull range (and few are, in these days of lawyer-designed rifles), it will need attention. Any trigger can be brought around by someone competent to do the work,

If the rifle's trigger doesn't break clean and crisp with little creep or overtravel, and if it is not in the 3- to 5-pound pull range, it will need attention. This RCBS scale will read the trigger pull of any rifle.

but if you don't have the ability, take the rifle to a qualified gunsmith.

If your stock lacks factory sling swivels, now is a good time to install them. Uncle Mike's sells swivels and studs for most any rifle made today. Uncle Mike's also sells a great set of drills made especially for this job, which come with complete instructions. A drill press is best, but if you have a good eye and a steady hand, you can install the studs with a hand-held electric drill. Always use a punch to mark the location before drilling, and be sure to seal the holes with glue to not only keep the studs in place, but to keep moisture out.

All metal surfaces of the rifle should be coated with either a quality, long-lasting chemical protector such as Outers Gunslick Metal Seal or a quality paste wax (the same as you'd use on your car).

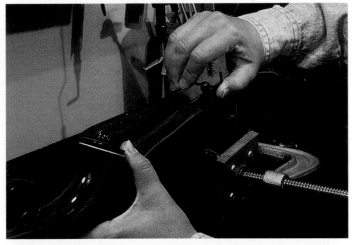

If your rifle does not have sling swivel studs, they're easy to install.

BACK TOGETHER AGAIN

Reassemble the rifle, being careful not to force anything. It might take a bit of patience to fit things together properly, so don't try to hurry the process. All screws should receive a

Screwdrivers should always fit exactly in the screws they are being used on.

drop or two of Loctite. I prefer the blue #242 because it allows the screws to be removed later. Snug up the action screws and then back them off slightly. Rap the butt of the rifle smartly on the floor a couple of times to settle the action against the bedding. (You did remember to replace the recoil pad, didn't you?) Now tighten the front action screw as tight as you can reasonably make it, and follow with the same on the rear screw. If your rifle has a center screw, leave it loose for now.

Visually check the stock for obvious twisting, warping or improper fit along the action and barrel. Alternately loosen and tighten each screw while watching the action for movement in the stock. By placing your fingers at the junction of the wood and metal, you can detect movement that your eye will miss. If any except the most minimal movement is detected, it may indicate a bedding problem. If you do have bedding problems, they must be corrected if you ever expect the rifle to shoot to its potential.

Finally, tighten the front screw and then the rear screw. The center screw should now be tightened snugly, but not as tight as the other two.

To check for adequate clearance with floating barrels, slide a dollar bill between the barrel and the stock. It should pass easily along the length of the barrel with no drag. On guns such as Remington's Model 700 BDL, there will be hard contact with the stock and barrel a few inches back from the front of the stock. You should be able to thread the dollar under the barrel behind this point. If the stock is hitting the barrel any place it should not, you must sand any high spots until you have the proper clearance. Don't forget to reseal the exposed wood.

Here's how to check for proper clearance between the wood and a floating barrel: The dollar bill should slide easily between the wood and metal with no drag. Any tighter fit must be relieved.

If you discover a bedding problem, there are several options that you or a gunsmith can choose, including glass bedding. If you fail to address this problem, it is likely that the rifle will never shoot as well as it should.

If you are going to use the rifle in cold weather, it is a good idea to disassemble the bolt and clean it with a good degreaser, such as Outers Crud Cutter. Relubricate the bolt with a modern product, such as Rem-Oil, that will not be affected by cold. Degrease the trigger mechanism with a spray, and lubricate sparingly.

Mount the scope according to the instructions found later in this chapter (see pages 88–91) and bore-sight it. The barrel will usually be dirty or full of shipping grease. Clean it thoroughly as explained later in this chapter (see "Cleaning a Rifle").

FIRST SHOTS

With a clean, dry barrel, fire three or four shots. If you fire from a good benchrest, you should have a group on the target. Adjust your scope as needed, and clean the barrel again,

The final step is to fire the rifle from a good solid bench rest to test ammo and zero the scope.

removing all copper fouling, until you have a clean, dry bore, and repeat the process. Continue until you have your groups centered where you want them.

Now you can proceed with testing to determine which load will best suit your needs. Remember to clean the barrel as detailed in the section on breaking in a bore (see "Breaking in a New Rifle Barrel"). Also, clean the barrel each time you switch ammo during your test. Fouling left in the bore from one brand of ammo or bullet can adversely affect the accuracy of the next brand you test.

If everything works and you are happy with the performance, then you and the rifle are ready for the field.

BREAKING IN A NEW RIFLE BARREL

"*I*s it necessary to break in a new rifle barrel? If so, how is it done? It seems confusing; is it important to follow the procedure exactly? Can doing it incorrectly ruin a new rifle? Help me, I'm so confused!"

I get a letter like that about once a month.

You may have read about the elaborate break-in procedures for rifle barrels that some gun writers are promoting. A few have come up with rigid schedules that they insist must be followed or you'll risk ruining the barrel. It all sounds mysterious and a little scary for somebody who has just laid out a bunch of cash for a new rifle.

IT'S NOT ROCKET SCIENCE

Relax—it's not that complicated, and it's hard to screw up. If you are properly caring for your rifle, you are probably close to doing it already. In the end, all you are doing in breaking in a rifle bore is using the bullets you are firing to burnish any minor imperfections in the rifling. Because those imperfections will collect metal fouling from the bullet jacket and "fill in," you must clean the fouling often and completely from the bore, particularly when the gun is new. If too many shots are fired between cleanings, the fouling can build up to the point where it will be difficult to completely remove. Removing the fouling after every couple of shots when the gun is new allows the next few bullets to burnish and polish the imperfections a little more before they start to fill in again. If the process is repeated often enough, the bore becomes "broken in" because it's smoother and the inevitable tool marks and other imperfections of the manufacturing process have been removed or reduced.

So how long do you continue? The rules aren't rigid, but the guidelines I loosely follow require that the bore be completely cleaned every two or three shots for the first 20 rounds fired through the rifle, then cleaned every five shots for the next 50 shots. After that, I clean as often as necessary.

"As often as necessary" means that the rifle should be cleaned before it's put away every time it is used. During use, it means to clean the rifle whenever accuracy starts to deteriorate or every 20 or so shots, whichever comes first. Every time the bore is cleaned, it continues the break-in process. Regardless of how you do it, the key is to completely remove all fouling each time and to do it often enough that the fouling doesn't have a chance to build up.

Bullet metal fouling is detrimental to accuracy in any rifle barrel. It is also a potential location for the beginnings of corrosion, which can pit and ruin a bore. Anything you can do to reduce fouling will be beneficial to the long-term accuracy and life of the rifle. The process is progressive—each time you clean a barrel, the subsequent bullets gradually smooth any minor imperfections left in the bore, leaving it a little smoother, a little better, a little more accurate. That doesn't mean that you can make a bad barrel win benchrest matches, but any barrel will benefit from this treatment.

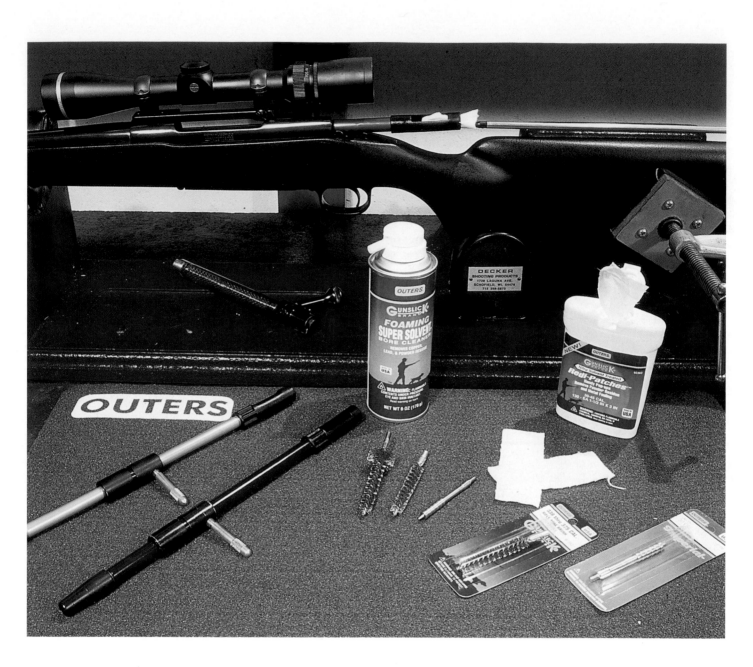

CLEANING A RIFLE

Y ou may think you have cleaned a rifle's barrel, but chances are that you have not done it correctly or completely. Running a few patches with some solvent through the barrel won't get the job done.

The truth is that a fouled bore is tough and time-consuming to clean properly, and because fouling is cumulative, each time that you fail to clean properly, the problem is compounded. Here are a few tips on how it's done.

BREECH IS BEST

There is an old saying that "more rifles are ruined by cleaning than are by shooting," and it's likely true. Cleaning rod wear, caused by the rod excessively contacting the rifling, is a common cause of barrel damage. This is particularly true when a cheap rod is used to clean from the muzzle. A soft aluminum rod picks up and embeds grit to become, in essence, a file that grinds away at the muzzle crown.

If it's possible, always clean from the breech and use a rod guide. The best guides not only keep the rod aligned with the bore but also protect the action from dripping solvent and crud. Bore guides also make it much easier to start a patch.

Some rifles, such as semiautos, lever actions or pump actions, must be cleaned from the muzzle. It is important in that situation to use a rod guide to align the rod with the bore and to protect the crown from cleaning rod wear. Also, put a rag in the action to catch the crud you push out of the barrel; you must keep that gunk out of the action.

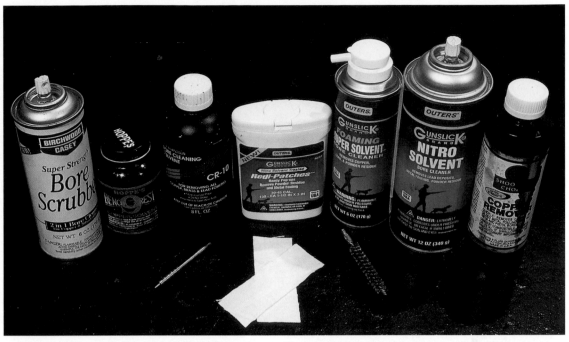

Other than elbow grease, the materials needed to clean a rifle bore are simple and inexpensive. You will need a general bore solvent and a good copper solvent. Be sure to read the instructions on the label; these are harsh chemicals.

THE PROPER PROCEDURE

It is always best to hold the rifle in a cradle of some sort when cleaning it. For a workbench, it is hard to beat the Decker Gun Vice. For fieldwork, such as at the range and also for the workbench, Midway offers a range box that serves for a multitude of chores in addition to carrying gear for the range. The box comes with a complete set of cleaning tools as well as a built-in cradle to hold the rifle. Those who have one of the ubiquitous MTM Shooter's Boxes might consider the MTM Portable Rifle Maintenance Center that will fit on top of the box for field cleaning.

Start cleaning the bore with a general bore solvent, making several passes through with a wet patch. Use each patch for only one pass before replacing it with a new solvent-soaked patch. You may want to let the gun soak a few minutes between patches to allow the solvent to work.

Leaving the barrel wet with solvent, use a properly fitted brush soaked with solvent to make several passes. Bronze is the best; nylon doesn't have the scrubbing ability, and stainless steel can gall and ruin the barrel very quickly. Keep the brush wet with solvent, reapplying after every couple of passes. Follow with one wet and several dry patches to remove all traces of solvent. After using the brush, always clean the solvent from it with a spray such as Outers Crud Cutter. This is to prevent abrasive debris from accumulating and also because some solvents will eat the bronze bristles.

The Right Cleaning Rod

*T*he best cleaning rods consist of one piece. Jointed rods have more flexibility, but the joints provide potential areas to collect embedded particles or sharp edges that can harm barrels. There are two schools of thought concerning the design of one-piece rods: some shooters like hardened steel rods, while others prefer plastic-coated rods. The theory is that a hard steel rod will not embed grit and become a "file." Other shooters prefer a coated rod because they believe that as a rod flexes inside the bore, it continuously hits the lands of the rifling. The theory is that a steel rod will continuously hit the barrel at the flex point and "peen" the rifling as it pushes the patch through, while a coated rod provides some protection against that. For what it's worth, most serious shooters I know use coated rods.

Now scrub the bore with a patch soaked with a good copper solvent. Be sure to read the instructions on the label because these are harsh chemicals. Let the bore soak for a few minutes, then follow with another patch wet with copper solvent. When you have patches coming out white with no

The 6 Commandments of Rifle Cleaning

1. Always clean a rifle as soon as possible after using it. The longer you leave the barrel dirty, the higher the potential for corrosion damaging the bore.

2. Use modern solvents that remove copper and powder fouling and keep cleaning until you have patches coming out white, indicating all fouling has been removed.

3. Always clean from the breech, if possible, using a bore guide. If you must clean from the muzzle, use a rod guide to protect the crown from damage.

4. Before storing a rifle for any length of time or after cleaning, always use a protectant on the bore and other exposed metal surfaces to prevent rust.

5. Before firing, always wipe the bore clean with a patch or two to remove any excessive residual oil.

6. Fire a fouling shot before hunting. Some rifles will shoot to a different point of aim with a clean bore than they will from a fouled bore. This is particularly true when there are traces of oil or other protectants in the bore.

trace of green or blue (it may take a while if the fouling is extensive), dry the bore with several clean patches.

Scrub the bore again with the general solvent, again using patches and brushes. Then dry and repeat the copper solvent treatment. Sometimes metal fouling can be trapped under layers of baked-on powder fouling that you must remove to allow the copper solvent to get at the metal fouling. Keep repeating this process until you have no sign of blue or green on any patches.

Cleaning the bore is made easier by the Foul Out Electronic cleaner from Outers. This device uses an electric current to activate a reverse-plating process that removes the fouling from the bore and deposits it on a metal rod, speeding up the process a great deal. The system is not terribly expensive, and anybody with several guns and an interest in shooting should have one. Use it where you would use the copper solvent.

Finally, dry the bore with several clean patches and apply a rust protector such as Outers Metal Seal. Before shooting again, run a dry patch through the barrel to remove any residual rust preventive. Often the first shot may be off from the group, usually high, so a fouling shot is not a bad idea before hunting.

The Outers Foul Out II electronic bore cleaner uses a reverse plating process to remove metal fouling from the rifle's bore and deposit it on a steel rod.

ACCURATE RIFLES & HOW TO ACHIEVE THEM

*T*he American way is to want the best, and there is certainly nothing wrong with that. It is that ever-reaching quest to be better that built this country, but sometimes we can become a little blinded by it.

Take today's rifles, for example. It would be hard to convince someone standing outside the shooting community and looking in that any rifle will shoot groups larger than minute of angle (M.O.A.). That magic number is all we hear when the talk is about rifles. We gun writers are the most guilty, and while it may harken back to Colonel Whelen's famous quote that "only accurate rifles are interesting," the truth is that nobody really wants to read about inaccurate rifles.

In our grandfathers' time, a rifle that would shoot to one M.O.A. was the holy grail of hunting guns; today it is almost the acceptable minimum. We are simply keeping pace. But should we demand one-inch groups at 100 yards for all our rifles?

Not if you want to remain sane.

In our grandfather's time, a rifle that would shoot to one M.O.A. was the holy grail of hunting guns. Today that is almost the acceptable minimum. But should we demand it from all our rifles?

DEFINING ACCURACY

Rifle designs and cartridge selection will dictate the inherent accuracy of any rifle. It is unreasonable to expect that a lever-action deer rifle will shoot as well as a bolt-action varmint rig. Nor should we expect that a .45-70 Gov. will shoot as accurately as a 6mm PPC. Certain cartridges have a lot more inherent accuracy than do others. That's not to say that the .45-70 Gov. is not capable of good accuracy, but it damn sure isn't in a league with the benchrest crowd, where the 6mm PPC dominated for many years.

My Remington 700 VS SV .22-250 will put good handloads into less than quarter-inch 100-yard groups, while my Ruger .44 Magnum Carbine struggles for two inches at half that distance, no matter what I feed it. But the point is that both are shooting to the best they are capable of, and there was a time when both rifles shot groups twice as large.

CREATING ACCURACY

With a little tinkering and attention to detail, almost any rifle can be made to shoot better. By using a few inexpensive tools, anyone who's reasonably handy can improve on the accuracy of a rifle. You don't need to be a trained machinist or a crotchety old gunsmith hermited away in a dusty shop to unlock a few secrets to better accuracy.

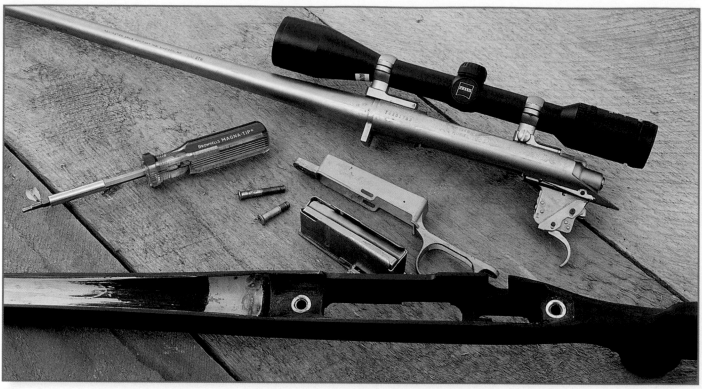

This rifle went from a very poor shooter to a very accurate rifle simply by pillar- and glass-bedding the action, filling the barrel channel of the stock to stiffen it, and floating the barrel.

Rifles are not entirely unlike people, and tastes for fuel can vary. For example, I kind of like broccoli, while many people do not; it's the same with guns. It is therefore assumed that you have already experimented with a variety of ammo, either factory or handloaded, to determine which one your rifle likes best.

Before doing anything else, clean the bore. An old gunsmith once told me that he believes a lot of the barrels that were replaced years ago as "shot out" probably just needed cleaning. The trouble was, back then they didn't have the super solvents and other cleaning tools we have today. It's a good thing that we have them, because fouling is in some respects a bigger problem now, particularly when shooting some of today's premium hunting ammo. The trend of high-performance cartridges with higher velocities and the specialized bullets that work best in these big cartridges can foul a barrel pretty quickly. Badly fouled barrels are never on accurate guns.

The next step would be to check all screws, including bedding and scope mounting screws, to be sure they are tight. Remove them one at a time and apply some Loctite before replacing. If the gun still refuses to shoot well, try another scope. It is not uncommon for even the best scopes to go bad.

COMMON CULPRIT: BEDDING

Poor bedding is a common problem with wooden stocks, but even synthetic stocks can fail. This is particularly true

with the cheaper injection-molded designs. Usually, it's a structural failure, such as a crack; however, I had one factory synthetic-stock gun that exhibited a tendency to string the shots vertically, a problem that got worse with use. A minor bedding problem was escalating as the rifle was used and barrel and action gradually compressed the stock. After I floated the barrel and glass-bedded the action, the groups shrank and became round instead of vertical.

You can sometimes detect bedding problems by holding the action with your fingers at the junction of the metal and wood and alternately loosening and tightening the action screws. Your fingers will feel movement that is undetectable to your eye, and anything more than minimal movement at all indicates a problem.

Another common bedding problem occurs when the stock is contacting the barrel improperly. To check for adequate clearance with floating barrels, wrap a dollar bill around the barrel with the ends pointing up and slide it along the barrel between the barrel and the stock. It should pass easily for the length of the barrel. The exception is that on some guns (including most Remington 700 rifles), there will be a deliberate hard contact a few inches back from the front of the forend. Any drag or sticking indicates that the stock may be contacting the barrel and affecting accuracy. Removing some material from the offending area will usually correct this problem. Also, sometimes in guns with a contact point near the forend tip, you will improve accuracy by removing that contact point for a fully floated barrel.

FIXING BEDDING PROBLEMS

Work carefully with sandpaper, a file or a small chisel. Go very slowly and remove only a little material at a time. Don't forget to seal any exposed wood with polyurethane to prevent water from causing the problem to recur.

Regardless of the cause, bedding-induced accuracy problems can usually be corrected by glass- or pillar-bedding the action and floating the barrel. Brownells has several bedding kits available.

When you are glass-bedding, the action and recoil lug area of the stock should be relieved to allow room for the bedding compound, leaving only a small support section behind the recoil lug and another for the receiver.

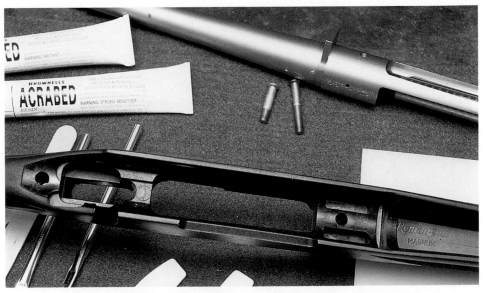

Regardless of the cause, bedding-induced accuracy problems can usually be corrected by glass- or pillar-bedding the action and floating the barrel.

The idea is to hold things in place until the bedding material has a chance to set up. If you are going to float the barrel, make sure that when the action is seated and the screws are snug you can pass a dollar bill without contact.

The front, sides and bottom of the recoil lug should be covered with a layer of masking tape before the release agent is applied. When the tape is removed, this creates a slight gap around the recoil lug, ensuring that the only contact is on

---

Screwdrivers

When working on guns, the importance of proper-fitting screwdrivers cannot be overemphasized. It may be the single most important factor in a good outcome when mounting a scope or doing any other gun work. The blades must be hollow- or parallel-ground and must fit the screw slot exactly. Several companies offer screwdrivers designed for use in working on guns. Here are a few I am familiar with.

One good one is Lyman's Magdriver with six hollow-ground bits, one 3/32 hex bit that are stored in the handle. Extra tips, including Phillips and Torx designs, are available. Suggested retail is $16.95.

Chapman has a couple of kits, the #9600 and the #8900, that include a screwdriver handle, an extension and a ratchet handle. Prices range from $16.95 to $29.95, depending on the kit.

Brownells has a huge variety of choices for screwdrivers, including the Chapman kits. In fixed-blade screwdrivers, the best is likely the Fixed-Blade Gunsmith Screwdrivers, which can be bought individually or in one of several sets. Individual prices average about $7.00, while the full kit costs $114.59. Other kits are available starting at about $60.

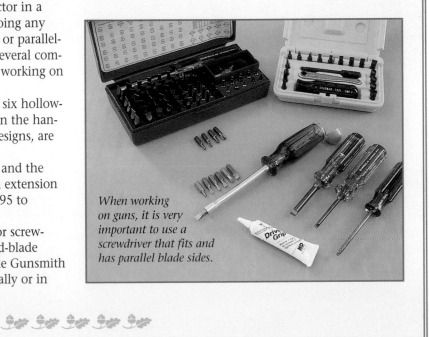

When working on guns, it is very important to use a screwdriver that fits and has parallel blade sides.

Triggers

Back in the days when gun companies used engineers instead of lawyers to design their rifles, a good trigger was expected on a new rifle. Not so today. Most of the rifles being shipped have triggers that are borderline horrible. It puzzles me why the gun makers think that a creepy, cruddy, 10-pound trigger is any more lawsuit-proof than a quality 4-pound trigger. As long as they both work properly and are safe, what's the difference?

At any rate, it's a rare factory rifle today that comes out of the box with a usable, let alone good, trigger. The sad fact is that no rifle will ever shoot to its potential without a decent trigger pull. The most accurate rifle in the world will have a hard time proving its accuracy if it's saddled with a rotten trigger.

It would simply be good policy with any new gun you buy to budget the price of a competent gunsmith fixing the trigger as part of the price.

Make sure the gunsmith is skilled, then ask for a trigger pull between 3 and 4 pounds on your big-game rifle. Request that it be smooth, with little creep and no overtravel. It will be the best thing you can do for your rifle and for your field shooting.

Then write a letter to the gun company and complain about the necessity of spending all that money and time before you can use your new $600.00 rifle. Don't expect an answer, but if enough letters show up maybe, just maybe, they will take note and start designing triggers right again.

the rear load-bearing surface. The entire action and the first 2 inches of the barrel are usually bedded at this time.

When the bedding agent has cured, remove the barrel action from the stock. (A little hint: If you put the gun in the freezer for a couple of hours before you separate the action and the stock, the metal will contract and make the job easier.)

If you are now going to glass the barrel channel, cover the barrel with two layers of 2-inch vinyl electrician's tape (don't forget the release agent) and then bed the length of the barrel. The tape serves as a spacer that, when removed, creates a gap and leaves the barrel free floating.

CROWN DAMAGE: CAUSE & CURE

One often-overlooked accuracy problem is caused by crown damage. Crown damage can rear its ugly head for many reasons, but one is quite common. The practice of carrying a rifle muzzle-down in a vehicle may have its foundation in safety, but it's torture to the delicate crown of any barrel. I cringe every time I see it being done. Grinding into the dirt and gravel that accumulates in any vehicle will act like an indiscriminate file to change the contours of the last part of the rifle any bullet touches before it begins its flight. An open bolt is just as safe and a lot easier on the rifle.

The simplest way to correct crown damage is with the inexpensive Brass Muzzle Crowning Lap from Brownells. Coat it with a good lapping compound and slowly rotate it on the crown with a variable-speed 3/8-inch drill while wobbling the tool, then do it in reverse. Wipe off the compound and check your progress often. When you have a clearly defined ring all around the muzzle and all the way to the bottom of the rifling lands, you are done. It's that simple. You might also consider using Brownells Muzzle Facing Tool with the appropriate pilot to cut a new crown and finish with a brass lapping tool that comes with it for a nice end product.

THE LAST STRAW

Finally, if you still can't make the gun shoot and there are no obvious defects, consider a new barrel. It doesn't happen all that often these days on big-game rifles, but it might be shot out.

Having done all these things, "poor accuracy" likely is out as an excuse for missing, so you will need to find a new one. "The wind" works for me.

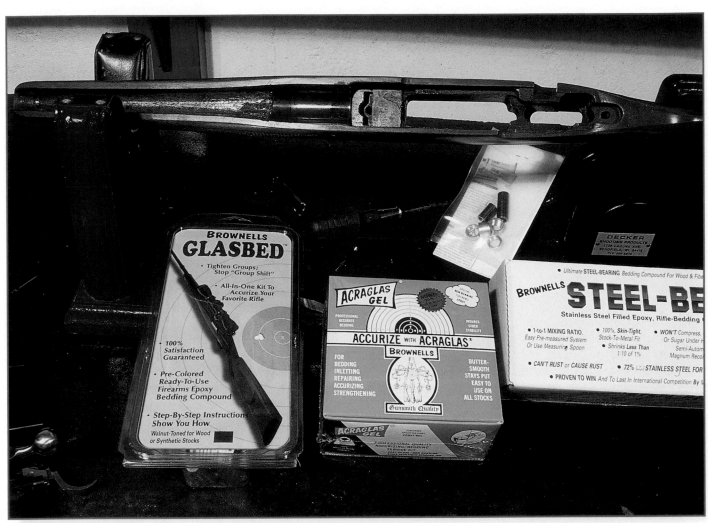

Simple jobs like rebedding a stock are easy for a home-based hobby gunsmith. Everything you need is available from the catalogs listed below.

Catalogs

There are at least four catalogs that any shooter should have.

Brownells Inc.
(Tools & gadgets)

Box 1
Route 2
200 South Front St.
Montezuma, IA 50171
(515) 623-5401

Midway Arms, Inc.
(Reloading & shooting supplies)

P.O. Box 718
5875 W. Van Horn Tavern Road
Columbia, MO 65203
(800) 243-3220

Sinclair International
(Precision shooting products)

2330 Wayne Haven St.
Ft. Wayne, IN 46803
(219) 493-1858

Stoney Point Products, Inc.
(Rod bore guides & other shooting products)

P.O. Box 234
1815 N. Spring St.
New Ulm, MN 56073-0234
(507) 354-3360

SCOPE-MOUNTING MADE EASY

*I*t is so rare to see a rifle in the field without a scope these days that everybody feels compelled to mention it. I hunted in northern Maine in 1997 with a Remington 7600 pump-action rifle mounted with a Williams peep sight. My choice was entirely intentional and made with good and sound reasoning. I was there to study the art of deer tracking with the legendary Benoit family, and because they believe that this setup is the best available for that style of hunting, I wanted to see firsthand if they were indeed correct. The question of whether they were right paled in comparison to the many times I had to explain why I didn't have a scope on my rifle. Everybody outside of the Benoits' circles that I ran into had to know. It would almost have been easier to have a card printed so I could hand it to people without needing to explain again verbally.

This only serves to illustrate that scopes are a fixture on today's hunting rifles. One primary factor in how well scopes perform is how they are installed. Improper installation can affect accuracy, reliability and even the life of the scope. It's not all that hard to do right, and with a minimum of tools,

anyone who is reasonably handy can mount a scope on a rifle so that everything works properly.

YOU NEED THE RIGHT TOOLS

As with any job, it is important to have the correct tools. Today, a lot of the mounts are using Allen head hex screws. These are an improvement over slotted screws, but they still strip if too much pressure is applied. The line between a tight screw and a stripped head is pretty fine, and care must be taken when tightening this—or any—style of mounting screw. Working with screws requires a wrench with clean, sharp edges that haven't been rounded by previous slippage during use.

Proper scope mounting requires a few special tools and attention to detail.

The current trend is to use Torx head screws. These require a special six-point star-shaped wrench that provides more gripping surface and allows more power to be applied to the screw without causing stripping.

Almost all gun work requires screwdrivers, and that includes a lot of scope mounts. Many mounts use slotted screws, and to the eyes of some shooters, these screws are still the most aesthetically pleasing. However, it is imperative that the proper screwdriver be used. The sides of the blade should either be hollow ground or have both sides parallel. Most screwdrivers sold in hardware stores have tapered sides and should never be used for working on guns. A screwdriver must fit exactly in the slot of the screw it is being used on, both in thickness of the slot and in the width of the screw. I cannot stress the importance of this enough. The reason is that a tapered or poor-fitting screwdriver will ride out of the slot as pressure is applied. This is guaranteed to not only ruin the screw, probably making it difficult to remove without drilling, but it can make the screwdriver fly off uncontrollably. This is, of course, dangerous, but will also add custom (although less than artistic) engraving to your rifle.

A product that I have found helpful when using screwdrivers or Allen wrenches is called Drive Grip (available from Brownells). It has fine abrasive in a gel carrier that, when applied to the contact surfaces between the screw and screwdriver or wrench, helps in gripping.

Another handy tool is a gun cradle to hold your rifle while you work. The first time you slip while trying to loosen a stubborn screw and stab your hand—or worse yet, gouge a chunk out of your rifle—you will agree.

GETTING READY

Before mounting the scope, you should clean all holes, contact surfaces, screws, rings and bases with a good degreaser. Most degreasers are nasty, so use them in a well-ventilated area. Protect your eyes and wash off any contact with your skin right away. You can also use isopropyl alcohol instead of a degreaser. I don't think this works quite as well, but it is a lot less offensive. If you do use a degreaser, the key is to use one that dries without any residue, leaving the metal clean.

"COVERING THE BASES"

Mount the base or bases on the receiver of the rifle, making sure to use the correct screws in the proper holes, because some bases use different-length screws in each hole. Leave all the screws loose and then tighten them one at a time, checking to see that the screw will tighten the base until you cannot move it. Then back out that screw and try the next one. This is to ensure that none of the screws is bottoming out instead of clamping the base.

Once you are sure all the screws will tighten the base properly, go ahead and snug them up. Alternate back and forth until all are as tight as you can reasonably get them with the tool you are using. This requires a balance and a certain feel. The screws must be tight, but you need to be careful not to strip them. Some sources recommend tapping the screwdriver with a hammer as you tighten the screw, but many now discourage this practice and I have found it unnecessary.

Leupold recommends that base screws be tightened to 20 inch-pounds and ring screws to 13 inch-pounds. As a guideline, Chapman says that with their screwdriver's relatively small handle and full hand pressure, most men will achieve 17 to 50 inch-pounds. With the thumb and first two fingers, most will apply 10 to 17 inch-pounds.

All screws should receive a drop or two of Loctite before installation. I prefer the blue #242 because it allows the

Adding LocTite to any gun screws is an important step. Make sure you use the kind that allows later removal of the screw.

screws to be removed later. I use a film of Loctite between the base and the receiver as well as a generous supply on the screws. After tightening the screws, clean off all excess Loctite. Don't forget to clean inside the action where the screw holes come through because the Loctite can drip through and cause problems if it's not cleaned up. At the same time, make sure that none of the screws is projecting past the end of the hole. If any are, take them out and recheck that you have the correct-length screws in each hole. If you find that the screws are placed correctly, grind or file a little off the end. Make sure to carefully bevel the end of the threads so that they will start into the holes properly.

Mounting the Rings

Now mount the rings on the bases. On dovetail turn-in type rings, add a bit more lubricant to the dovetail before

Use a 1-inch aluminum rod to turn in a dovetail ring. Never use the scope itself.

installing the ring. Never use the scope to turn the rings into place. Instead, use a 1-inch aluminum or wooden rod or a Leupold Ring Wrench. If you use a rod, always have the tops of the rings screwed on before you apply torque to avoid springing the bottom ring, causing the top to misalign. If this happens, you will have trouble starting the screws and the ring won't fit the scope right.

Use the rod to make sure that both rings are aligned properly before you install the scope. If you can lay the rod in the rings and turn or slide it back and forth without any of the edges or corners shaving or dragging and the rod lies on the

Here's how to use a 1-inch aluminum rod to check the alignment of the two scope rings.

bottom of both rings, you have them properly aligned. Better still, if you are going to mount more scopes over the years, buy a set of scope alignment rods or sleeved scope alignment rods (for use on 30mm as well as 1-inch rings) from Brownells. These are pointed on one end, and after mounting one in each ring, you adjust the rings until the points are in perfect alignment with each other.

Proper alignment between the two scope rings insures that the scope is not stressed during installation. Sleeved scope alignment rods from Brownells will work with 30 mm as well as 1-inch rings. Line up the points, and the rings are in perfect alignment with each other.

Lap the Rings

After you have the rings in alignment, it is a good idea to lap them. (Lapping uses a mild abrasive and a one-inch, or 30mm, steel rod to remove the high spots and bring the rings into perfect alignment with each other.) Due to variances in manufacturing the rings and gun receivers, there can be some subtle differences between the front and rear rings. Lapping eliminates those differences. This improves the mounting job and adds to the gripping surface, which can be important for hard-recoiling guns.

Both Brownells and Sinclair International offer ring-lapping kits. They are simple to use. Coat the rod with compound and place it in both rings. Now move it back and forth while rotating slightly and applying downward pressure. Check often to see how much of the ring is being lapped, and stop when you have about 75 percent contact on both ring bases. It is not necessary to lap the tops of the rings.

I often use a film of Loctite on both sides of the rings to help in adhesion. This is unnecessary on most guns, but on hard-recoiling guns it adds a little insurance. Loctite is, however, hard to remove if you take the scope off.

Lapping the scope rings allows a more even contact with the scope. Here is the Sinclair International lapping tool in use. Note the lapping compound in the small white container.

SCOPE & CROSSHAIRS

After placing the scope in the rings, tighten the screws until there is a little drag on the scope but so you can still move it. Adjust the scope forward and back until the eye relief is correct for you. With a variable scope, make certain that you check it at both ends of the power spectrum.

Perhaps the most difficult part of mounting a rifle scope is aligning the crosshairs. The vertical crosshair should be in line with the axis of the bore, but on a huge number of rifles

that I look at, it's tilted. This can make it difficult to properly sight in your rifle and can even affect your shooting in the field. The Reticle Leveler from Segway Industries solves that problem. It's one of those "why didn't I think of that?" gadgets. It indexes to a flat surface, usually on the base, and allows alignment of the crosshairs with the bore. It is remarkably easy to use and surprisingly accurate. When the crosshairs are aligned correctly, tighten the ring screws in an alternate pattern, left to right and front to back.

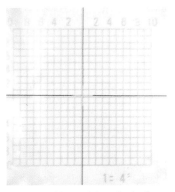

An optical bore sighter is the best way to get your rifle on target. The scope's crosshairs are centered on the bore sighter's grid, and that usually will place the bullet's impact on the target. Make the final adjustment by shooting from a solid rest.

FINE DETAILS

When you cleaned the mounts, you left the metal without protection, so now is a good time to spray the rings and bases with a metal preservative or oil to prevent rusting. Be careful not to get any on the lenses; you don't want any oil on the optics.

I have used this method of installing scopes on rifles up to .375 H&H Mag. without a single problem. However, in really hard-kicking rifles, you might consider epoxy on the

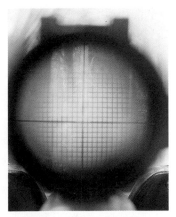

Here's the view as you use a bore sighter to adjust the scope enough to "get it on the paper."

bases and epoxy, rosin or another grip enhancer on the rings. Just remember that epoxy is pretty permanent—you can remove it with heat, but that's difficult and tricky when you have optics involved.

Bore sighting can be accomplished by clamping the rifle, minus the bolt, in your cradle and sighting through the bore at a distant object. Then, without moving the rifle, turn the scope adjustments until the crosshairs are centered on the same object. A much easier way, in fact the only way, for rifles such as lever actions that don't allow you to look through the breech is to use a commercial bore sighter. Just remember, though, bore sighting is only to "get you on the paper." You must shoot the rifle to completely sight in the rifle.

If you follow these simple instructions, you should have years of trouble-free service from your scope and rifle.

And a lot fewer questions to answer.

REMOVABLE MOUNTS & OTHER NECESSARIES

When I was a kid growing up in the '60s, it seemed like everybody I knew who had a scope on his deer rifle also had a backup system. November weather in New England is some nasty stuff, and it wasn't a question of if a scope was going to fog up, but when.

Looking back, I see that perhaps a lot of it was because we were mostly poor, and an expensive, high-quality scope was as rare in our woods as a big 10-point buck. But, regardless of the reasons, it certainly left an impression on the deer-hunting psyche of the area, and even today, many hunters refuse to buy a rifle without iron sights, even if they plan to mount a scope. One hunter I know has even had new rifles drilled and tapped for backup sights.

While fogging scopes are rare today in comparison to 30 years ago, most of the rifle failures I have witnessed in hunting camps in recent years have still been caused by the scopes. Usually this is because of damage, not scope failure. Because optics require relatively fragile construction when compared to the rifle, they remain the weak link of any hunting gun setup. The ability to easily remove and change sighting systems in the field makes sense.

SOME GOOD REMOVEABLE MOUNTS

A very popular scope mount is the Weaver Pivot Mount. When in the shooting position, the scope is held in place with spring steel lips that grip the base. Using the hinge that opposes the lips, you can quickly pivot the scope to the side to use the iron sights. Another twist of the wrist and the scope is returned to shooting position.

The ever-popular Weaver Detachable Top Mount (and its many clones) is another excellent removable mount. One excellent variation on this is Leupold's QRW all-steel rings and mounts. A twist of the knob or lever and each ring is set free. I have these rings on many guns, including several muzzleloaders, from which the rings come off each time I clean the guns.

Leupold's Quick Release uses rings fitted to the base by means of pins with half-circle cuts in them. There is a cross-pin in the base that is milled to accept the rings. When turning those cross-pins with the levers on the side, the round section pivots to mate with the milled section of the ring pins, locking them together. Turning the levers in the other direction releases the rings, and the scope is lifted off the base. I have this mount on my Remington 700 in .35 Whelen. I have two scopes set in rings and zeroed, a Leupold 2.5-8X and a Nikon 1.5-4.5X. With them, I have the option of matching the scope to the terrain. I can also zero each for a different load. With two scopes and the iron sights, I am pretty well secure that I will have something to aim my rifle with when it comes time to shoot.

Warne Manufacturing Company has some of the finest detachable mounts currently available. The mounts use an almost petite base with grooves to accept the rings. There are lugs on the rings that fit into cuts on the bases to take the

Removable scope mounts allow this rifle to have two different scopes zeroed and ready to use. This allows for a backup in case of failure and also lets you change scopes for differing conditions.

recoil. The rings are attached to the bases with levers that act as wrenches. Pull them against a spring, and they can be turned independently of the nut they tighten. Let them back down, and they turn the nuts to loosen or tighten them.

After fairly extensive testing, I can say that the point-of-impact changes when removing and replacing scopes are detectable, but barely. It is so small as to be completely irrelevant to most hunting use.

As a frequent victim of Murphy's Law, I appreciate the options these mounts provide. Because they must be held to such close tolerances, most of them are not inexpensive, but any serious user I know considers it an insurance payment.

NOISY STOCKS

A lot of injection-molded synthetic rifle stocks have hollow butts that are noisy. The empty space acts as a sound chamber and amplifies the sound, which may have turned off a lot of hunters to "plastic" on their rifles. The best solution I have found is to fill the space with those ubiquitous Styrofoam peanuts that are used in shipping.

Remove the recoil pad and cram the stock full. Really work the peanuts in, crushing and crunching until you fill the space with as much foam as you can, then replace the recoil pad. This adds only a few ounces, but it quiets that hollow sound so common to these stocks.

CASES

Airline baggage handlers have an inherent hatred for gun cases (I believe it's a condition for employment). They see it as their mission in life to destroy anything that might possibly hold a gun. Those plastic cases, while tough, are flexible. This allows any impact to telegraph to the contents. The foam liners cushion the blow, but the first solid material the

energy meets is the rifle. The plastic shell has a memory that returns all but the hardest hits to its original shape, masking that the event even occurred. The hunter does a cursory damage exam and concludes that all is well. Then the hunter misses the buck of a lifetime before discovering that the scope's zero was knocked a foot off from where it was expected to shoot.

The answer is in a quality aluminum case. Tougher than any plastic box, aluminum cases provide a

Gun cases get beat up in airline transport. The only answer: a quality aluminum case.

rigid, hard shell that will not flex under impact, transmitting less of any hit to the enclosed gun. The dents will tell you how mad the baggage handler was at your particular case, and they will let you know when something serious has happened. You should always check your zero, but big dents make it even more important to do so.

Good protection starts a good trip, and money spent on a quality gun case will keep you happy when you arrive.

Springy Slings

If you haven't already, give a neoprene rifle sling a try. I have been using them for years, often with some pretty chunky rifles, and I am impressed. Not only do they grip your shoulder, keeping the rifle in place, but they reduce the perceived weight as well. The stretchy rubber-like material acts as a shock absorber as you walk, and the rifle seems a lot lighter.

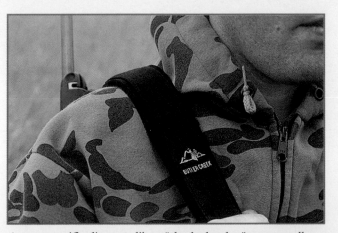

A neoprene rifle sling acts like a "shock absorber" as you walk, and reduces the perceived weight of the rifle.

Chapter 5

THE SHOT

*I*t's a mixture of art, science, skill, magic, physics, athleticism, mysticism and mystery. We call it shooting, and ever since man learned to make objects fly through the air, we have been trying to do it better.

Rifle shooting skill has long been admired by strong men and swooned over by pretty ladies. Before part of our "enlightened" society deemed guns to be "evil" and all shooting out of fashion, it was a skill all American heroes possessed.

There was a time when crowds flocked to see Annie Oakley and other exhibition shooters dazzle and amaze spectators with their skill. American history is filled with men who possessed legendary shooting skill: Daniel Boone, Davy Crockett, Jim Bridger, Buffalo Bill Cody, Wild Bill Hickock and so many others. Men who lived by the rifle, such as Theodore Roosevelt, were elected president. They became enduring heroes because they could shoot.

Even our pretend heroes rode to prominence on shooting skills; John Wayne and Clint Eastwood rarely missed and always outshot the bad guys.

Shooting well is still a skill that's admired in the circles I prefer to travel in and by those people who quietly continue to make this country great. Here are some of the secrets.

SHOOTING WELL

Ninety percent of rifle shooting is mental. The rest, of course, is physical, but to think you can master one without the other is pure folly. Sure, your muscles support the rifle, and that's physical. But the key is in holding it in a way that allows you to hit your target. That part is mental. You must use your brain to control the rifle, your emotions, your thoughts and your body. That's a lot tougher than simply holding an 8-pound rifle.

In teaching the basics of shooting, most instructors try to make the trigger release and the shot firing a surprise to the shooter. That's a good technique as far as it goes. It sets the stage for the mental aspect of good shooting, but to be a truly good shot, you must take it beyond that point. This is partic-ularly true when field shooting at game. The best shooters, particularly the best game shots, know exactly when the trigger will break and the rifle will fire. However, it takes a lot of focused practice at shooting to achieve that skill level.

PRACTICE WORKS

You must have a disciplined, methodical and linear approach to practice. Start by practicing the basics of shooting from a target-shooting perspective. Good shooting is good shooting, regardless of what the bullets are hitting, and to learn to shoot well you must punch some paper so you can see the bullet hole locations and assess what is happening.

The fundamentals of target shooting are the foundation

It's a mixture of art, science, skill, magic, physics, athleticism, mysticism and mystery. We call it shooting and ever since man learned to make objects fly through the air we have been trying to do it better.

for good field shooting, and it's there you must start. As covered later in this chapter, you should start by shooting off a solid bench with sandbags until you are comfortable with the techniques and then progress to practicing from field positions (see page 106 in "Learning to Deal with Recoil").

THE RIGHT SIGHT PICTURE

Regardless of the position, the basic technique is to hold a constant sight picture, that is, the alignment between the front and rear sights. When using a modern scope, this is a moot point because there are no front and rear sights, only the crosshairs, which are a single visual plane with your eye and the target, so hunters with scopes can skip this step. If you are using iron sights, you must learn to maintain constant and correct sight alignment.

With any shooting position, the rifle will have some movement, although the amount will vary with the position, type of rest and the skill of the shooter. Movement will be minimal when shooting from a good benchrest and most obvious when you are shooting offhand. Regardless of the

position and the amount of rifle wobble, you must learn to control that movement.

At a media shooting event before the Shooting, Hunting, Outdoor Trade (SHOT) Show in Atlanta one year, several

You must have a disciplined, methodical and linear approach to practice. Start by practicing the basics of shooting from a solid bench until you are comfortable with the techniques.

"It's simple. Control the sight wobble until it is staying on the center of the target, then squeeze the trigger!" Practice the technique enough and you too will become a good game shot.

writers and industry people were watching Winchester's Mike Jordan shooting a rifle offhand at a 300-yard gong. Someone asked him how he could hit it almost every time.

"It's simple: Control the sight wobble until it is staying on the center of the target, then squeeze the trigger!"

YOU WON'T GET IT ALL PERFECTLY STILL

I am not sure I agree it's all that simple, but Mike is certainly right. Most new shooters think that the secret is in holding the sights perfectly still on the target until the shot. But any experienced shooter will tell you that Superman couldn't hold a rifle perfectly still, particularly from field positions. If you concentrate all your focus on keeping the

crosshairs exactly where you want the bullet to hit, you are never going to shoot well. They will move back and forth across the target, and you will find yourself yanking the trigger whenever the sights are on the bull's eye. Do that and you will miss every time.

Instead, while maintaining the sight alignment, confine the sights' (and subsequently the rifle's) movement to a circle. The better you get at doing this, the smaller the circle grows, but it takes practice and discipline. Part of that practice is building muscle memory, and there are no real shortcuts. The best shooters can control the "cone of movement" to an area smaller than the X-ring on the target. To hit the X-ring every time, the sights must not only be wobbling in an area smaller than the X-ring but also smaller than the accuracy potential of the rifle. That is, if the rifle shoots 1-inch groups at that distance and the X-ring is 2 inches, the cone of movement must be less than 1 inch to ensure hitting the X-ring every time.

Even from a benchrest, you will likely have a very small amount of movement. It's almost impossible not to; the human body is a dynamic machine that's always in motion. You must breathe, and blood must pump through your muscles. If you are to control the rifle and make it fire, you must move muscles, tendons and ligaments. It is impossible to do this without some influence on the rifle. Simply put, if you are touching the rifle in any way, you will be inducing movement. The secret is in controlling that movement, penning it up, so to speak, so that its influence is minimized or turned to your advantage.

FOCUS ON THE TARGET

Your mental focus during the shot should be on sight alignment and controlling the cone of wobble, not on the trigger. Breathe naturally as you prepare for the shot. As the cone of wobble settles and you are nearing the shot, exhale about two-thirds of your last breath and stop breathing. Holding your breath like this will allow you several seconds to take the shot before you start to feel the

effects of oxygen deprivation. If you cannot shoot quickly enough, breathe again until you feel the need receding, then repeat the process. Don't try to wait out the need to breathe; you can't. You will rush the shot and miss. Once that need is present, it will destroy your chances for a good shot. Stop adding pressure to the trigger, breathe, then start again.

As you focus on keeping the sights' wobble on the center of the target, slowly and evenly increase the tension on the trigger. If the sights move out of the target zone, stop increasing the tension, but don't let up on the trigger. As the sights move back onto the target zone, start increasing trigger pressure again. Always apply trigger pressure in a slow, even and progressive manner. It takes discipline to fight the urge to jerk or yank the trigger when the sights are on the bull's eye; that's where the mental part comes into play. You must apply pressure to the trigger slowly, progressively and continuously until the rifle fires.

SQUEEZE THE TRIGGER

At this point, the gun firing should come as a surprise. However, if the sights are controlled to within the target zone (the X-ring on a bull's eye target or the center of the kill zone on a big game animal) and you correctly follow through, the bullet will strike that zone.

If you try to pull the trigger only when the sights are centered

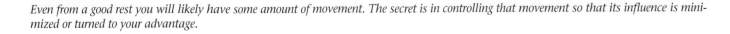

Even from a good rest you will likely have some amount of movement. The secret is in controlling that movement so that its influence is minimized or turned to your advantage.

on the bull's eye, you will tend to yank the trigger and pull the rifle away from the target before the bullet exits the barrel. Besides, with the reaction lag from both the shooter and the rifle, the sights will likely have wandered off from the target by the time the bullet exits the barrel. Either way, you will miss. It's better at this point to have the rifle firing as a surprise. That ensures that you are smoothly and gradually increasing pressure on the trigger so that the pull is not disturbing to the sight picture. If you are properly controlling the sight wobble, the shot will be good.

Follow-through is very important as well. You should never look past the sights to see the bullet strike or react to the shot in any other way. Instead, keep your focus on the sights, target and trigger until well past the shot. While it takes only a millisecond for the bullet to exit, that's enough time to wreck the shot if follow-through is not adhered to properly.

As your skill progresses, you will find two things happening: First, that the process happens much faster, and second, that the trigger releasing no longer comes as a surprise. The best shooters are so in tune with their rifle and the shooting process that they know and control exactly when the shot is fired.

Secrets from an Expert

During the 1996 Olympics in Atlanta, I worked as a press information liaison for the shooting events at Wolf Creek.

This job gave me relatively unfettered access to the shooters, and I found talking with them informally to be the best way to learn a few of their secrets. During a break on one of the practice days, I was sitting and talking with Rajmond Debevec from Slovenia. At that time, Rajmond was the world record holder for both 50-meter free rifle three-position shooting and 10-meter air rifle. At 33 years old, this was his fourth Olympic competition, and the list of his world-class competitions read like a book.

If there is a shooting sport that epitomizes the concept being explored here, it is Olympic rifle shooting. To win, shooters must not only hit a tiny X-ring, but in the case of the air rifle shooter, an X-ring that's considerably smaller than the pellet they are shooting. They must center the hit on the X-ring to score the bonus tenths of a point that separate gold from the rest. They must do it while standing in many of the rifle competitions.

I noticed Rajmond was shooting a new model of .22 LR rifle, and I asked him how he liked it.

"It's more accurate than the gun I was using before, and that's good, but to tell you the truth, I don't like it as well," he said.

When I asked why, he explained that the barrel was 2 inches longer on this rifle, and the added time the bullet was in the barrel was hurting his scores. He actually was in such full control of the rifle that he based his timing of the shot

Your mental focus during the shot should be on sight alignment and controlling the cone of wobble.

While most of us will never achieve the control level of an Olympic champion, it is desirable to reach a point where you are in control of the rifle and the shot.

on where the sights would be when the bullet exited the barrel and was no longer influenced by the rifle. The slightly increased bullet time in this longer barrel was causing him some problems.

Of course, Olympic-style competition is won and lost by thousandths of an inch, while big game shooting is not as critical, but the point is that Rajmond was incredibly in tune and in control of his rifle. You can bet that he knew exactly when the trigger would release for each and every shot. I don't know if Rajmond is a hunter, but if he is, I'll bet he is just as deadly in the field as he is on the target range.

STAY IN CONTROL

While most of us will never achieve the control level of an Olympic champion, it is desirable to reach a point where you are in control of the rifle and the shot. You will know you are approaching this point when you start to "call" the shots. If you make a poor shot, you will know instantly where the bullet went and why without looking. A check of the target should confirm what your brain saw, and the bullet will likely have struck where you called that it would.

You can't will yourself to this point; you have to arrive at your own pace. Practice the technique that has the gun firing as a surprise enough, and one day you will realize that it's not a surprise any more, that you know exactly when the rifle will fire. You can't force it, so don't try. Just keep practicing until it happens on its own. You will find that your shooting has improved through this, and by then you should be shooting very well.

It is only after you have arrived at this point of rifle and trigger control when shooting from any position that you will truly become a good game shot.

THE KEY TO GOOD SHOOTING IS IN THE BENCH

*I*n my business, I get to talk with a lot of outfitters. From bear guides in the thick Northeast to pronghorn hunters in the open plains of the West, they all have a common complaint about hunters who cannot shoot well.

It is not an American heritage inherent to our breeding to be a crack shot. Even Davy Crockett had to practice! Back in my competitive shooting days, I had the good fortune of meeting and competing with some of the best shots on Earth. They did not get that way by luck; every single one gathered the skills by practicing! The old myth of "I can't hit paper but I am deadly on game" is just not true. The really good shots hit what they shoot at, no matter what the composition.

"ONE CHANCE" MEANS "PRACTICE NOW"

It amazes me that a hunter will spend so many days and dollars in the quest for a buck yet neglect the most important aspect, the very thing he is working for: the shot. A chance at a trophy animal is too rare an opportunity to blow it for something so easily controlled, yet year after year it continues to happen.

Your chance, if it comes at all, may be fleeting and not repeated. You may have to shoot fast and well, and there is no substitute for practice. So burn some powder before the season. Sure, ammo is expensive, but missing the trophy of a lifetime will make it seem cheap in retrospect.

But before you go out and start blasting, you must make sure that your practice will work to improve your shooting and not just help you to get better at bad habits. It will do you no good to keep repeating the same mistakes over and over; this will only make it that much harder to unlearn them. Regardless of your present ability, it is best to start at the beginning of a shooting improvement program. If you skip a step, it may show up in problems later.

While it is often stated that shooting from a bench has no practical benefit for the hunter, I strongly disagree. Shooting from any position is poor practice if the same mistakes are repeated over and over and you don't realize you are making them. Learn the basics of shooting from a bench, where the human factor can be minimized. Practice the fundamentals of sight picture, breath control and trigger pull from a bench with a solid rest. When you can regularly shoot groups approaching the rifle's capabilities, then progress to field positions.

KNOW YOUR RIFLE

A rifle's capabilities often remain a mystery, even to long-time owners. Determining the best groups from a rifle takes an experienced shooter, and if you have progressed to that level, then you probably don't have any reason to be reading

this. There will come a time when you know the rifle well enough to recite its accuracy capabilities, but for now, you need something to measure by. Any factory rifle today should be able to shoot five shot groups of 3 inches or better (usually much better) at 100 yards. Most newer bolt actions should shoot groups half that size. Until you can do that well or better with every group you fire, then you should stay at the shooting bench and continue to work on the fundamentals.

WORKING FROM THE BENCH

Before you start, it's a good idea to take the rifle to a gunsmith to make sure that all screws are tight. This should include all bedding screws as well as all the scope mounts. Then have the gunsmith bore-sight the gun. Next, go to a good 100-yard range with a solid shooting bench. If you don't know where there is one, ask your gunsmith or at the local gun shop about joining a local Fish & Game club, because they usually have a shooting range available. If you absolutely cannot find a range with a bench, there are several portable benches on the market you can bring with you.

Follow the instructions in the section on sighting in the rifle ("The Correct Way to Sight In a Rifle" in Chapter 6) until you have it hitting where you want it to at 100 yards.

This shooter is using improper technique. He is off balance and not using the bench to support his body correctly. His hand is holding the front of the rifle and the rear is supported by his body rather than a sandbag rest.

Now, fire five shots as carefully as you can. It is advisable to pad your shoulder; it won't make you a wimp but will improve your shooting. I use athletes' elbow pads: one for most rifles, two for the big guys. PAST makes commercial pads that work extremely well. You also might consider a muzzle brake, either an add-on or the Mag-Na-Port style that doesn't alter the barrel length. Always wear hearing protection; that too will help in the flinch department as well as preserve your hearing.

At this point, don't worry about where you are hitting as long as it's somewhere on the target. Your five holes should be relatively close together, say, 3 inches or less. If they are not, then you are flinching or the gun is not accurate with the ammo you are using. Continue to try, and if you just can't make the group size shrink, try different ammo. If you still cannot find the problem, it may take another, more experienced shooter trying your rifle to discover why it isn't grouping. Be forewarned, though, it's almost always the shooter!

By firing five shots, you can tell if you begin to flinch. If you do and the groups open up, it's advisable to stop shooting for the day and give it a rest because all you will do from then on is burn shells and heat up your temper. Go back another day and start again fresh.

DON'T GIVE UP

The best practice at this point is to continue to shoot from the bench until you can shoot to the rifle's capability on demand. It may take several weeks of shooting before you reach this point, and if you still don't know what that capability is, then you haven't shot enough groups from your rest.

I can't stress enough the importance of mastering the fundamentals before you attempt to go on to practicing field positions. Don't expect to learn it all in one session. If you are starting to find your concentration wandering and your groups opening up, call it a day. You can't force yourself to overcome it, and you will only be frustrated and conditioning yourself to bad habits. Stop while you are shooting well and end the day on a positive note; it makes it easier to maintain the mental attitude and determination needed to learn the shooting skills.

After you have mastered the fundamentals, then you can progress to practicing from field positions. However, take a trip back to the shooting bench every now and then to make sure you are not picking up some bad habits or forgetting the basics of good shooting.

It will do you no good to keep repeating the same mistakes over and over. Learn the basics of shooting from a bench, where the human factor can be minimized. Only then can you determine your rifle's true accuracy potential.

LEARNING TO DEAL WITH RECOIL

*I*f you think that guiding hunters for a living is a cushy job, then I'll wager you have never done it. Finding the game is the easy part. It's dealing with some of the hunters you get that is difficult. You have to be a buddy, baby-sitter, instructor and diplomat all in one. But the most universal complaint from guides is about clients who miss. (That's where the diplomat part comes into play.)

It may well be the epitome of frustration when, after a long week of hard hunting, you finally have that elk (or deer, turkey, moose or whatever) right in front of your client. It's a chip shot, a slam dunk, a sure thing—but still, the hunter misses clean. You try to be nice and say it wasn't really his or her fault, making up some excuse like the wind or the critter moved just as the shot was fired. But then,

somehow or other, by the end of the hunt it always turns around and becomes your fault that the hunter didn't get the game.

Oh, well, it still beats a real job.

CULPRIT: RECOIL

Several things contribute to the preponderance of misses. But other than a lack of practice, the top reason is fear of recoil. If you are scared of your gun, you will never shoot it well. Many hunters are lugging guns that are too big for them. Perhaps a buddy or even some gun writer has him convinced that he needs a big magnum, but often the scenario follows another well-established pattern. Hunters

This shooter is using a sandbag between his shoulder and the rifle. This helps reduce the felt recoil from the big Remington .300 Ultra Mag.

.338 Mag. to kill a deer, or any other critter in North America for that matter, except maybe a grizzly bear. There is nothing wrong with a magnum if you can handle it well, but many hunters cannot. Don't let your ego override your good sense here. A solid hit with a .280 Rem. is a lot better than a miss—or worse, a wounding shot—with a .338 Win. Mag. Do not overcompensate, though, and make the mistake of choosing an inadequate caliber simply because of a fear of recoil. The loss of a wounded animal is inexcusable when it could have been prevented, and by using inadequate calibers, you are courting disaster.

The next key to conquering recoil—and there's no short-cut—is to practice shooting. Practice a little bit, lots of times. Don't keep shooting until it hurts; quit while it's still fun. Just make sure you do it often enough to realize that the recoil really isn't all that bad and that shooting is really a lot of fun.

Start by initially shooting from a benchrest. This will give you the ability to control any recoil while you familiarize yourself with the gun. It will also allow you to test your ammo for accuracy and to adjust the rifle's zero correctly.

My method is to use an Uncle Bud's bench bag for the front bag. When properly used, it grips the fore-end of the gun and holds against the recoil. The rear of the gun is supported by a Bench Wizard bag from Ultra Light Arms. This features two 5-pound sandbags connected by a webbing that fits around the rear of the gun to effectively add the weight of the bags to the gun. Another 10-pound sandbag is placed against the rear of this bag, and I use a PAST Shooting Pad between the gun and my shoulder. All this effectively controls recoil of most any rifle. Using these methods, I have been able to conduct long test sessions of several hundred rounds at a time with hard-recoiling rifles such as the .375 H&H Mag.

Another good product is the Bench Master rifle rest from Desert Mountain Manufacturing. It is a one-piece rifle rest that holds the rear of the gun with a web across the butt pad and helps to reduce recoil by adding the 9-pound weight of the rest to the rifle. You can add some sandbags across the frame for even more weight.

never like to admit to a miss, and they will convince themselves that they hit that critter. Maybe they even did, but in a nonlethal place. Either way, it's not their fault (in their minds), so it must be that their present guns aren't big enough. So, they upgrade to bigger magnums that scare the hell out of them. They won't practice because they don't like to shoot them, and when they do, they are so scared of the things that they flinch like they are expecting a right cross from Evander Holyfield.

I know one New England deer hunter who bought a .458 Win. Mag. because he lost a white-tailed deer he hit with his .338 Win. Mag. (which he bought to replace the .30-06 that "wasn't big enough for those tough Maine bucks"). When pushed, he admitted that he hit the buck in the back leg, but that didn't change his mind; he thought it would have died with the .458 Win. Mag. This guy is trying to substitute firepower for skill and practice, and he is hardly alone. It's a common story.

RECOIL REMEDIES

The first solution to managing recoil is to be reasonable in your choice of calibers. You simply don't need a big .300 or

This Bench Wizard sandbag wraps around the butt of the gun, adding weight and reducing recoil.

The length of pull is the distance from the trigger to the butt. This factor in stock fit can make a difference in felt recoil. Also, synthetic stocks help reduce felt recoil.

Once you have mastered the nuances of your rifle from the bench, take your practice shooting to field positions. You will be amazed at how much you have improved simply by having fired a lot of ammo under the carefully controlled conditions of a bench. Just be sure to go back to the bench every now and then to see if you are developing any recoil-induced bad habits.

OTHER RECOIL FACTORS

There *are* things you can do to make the perceived recoil of your rifle more pleasant. The first and foremost is to buy a heavy gun. The laws of physics being what they are—"for every action there is an equal and opposite reaction" and all that—the heavier the gun, the less it reacts to the equal and opposite reaction. Depending on your hunting style, a gun that weighs a pound or two more may be the deciding factor. This is fine for hunting in a Texas deer blind, but you can come to hate that extra pound by the end of a 10-day elk hunt in the steep mountains. There are other considerations as well.

Stock fit and design are important to "perceived" recoil; that is, how you are feeling the recoil of your particular rifle. Any stock that doesn't fit well will hurt. Length of pull is important, and according to Donald Gemes, formerly with the custom shop at Reinhart Fajen, Inc. and now owner of Show Me Gun Stocks, the correct length of pull will have about an inch of clearance between the thumb of the trigger hand and the shooter's nose. This should also put the forearm of the trigger arm at about a 30-degree angle to the rifle.

The final determining factor is always the way the stock feels to the shooter. Gemes adds that, with an ill-fitting stock, it is often the face that is beat up more than the shoulder and that a comb that is parallel to the bore or tapered slightly

Finding a Flinch

No shooter flinches.

At least not if the shooter gets to tell the story.

Any time a rifle is scattering shots around the target, particularly low and left, suspect a flinch. Surprisingly, some shooters flinch so consistently that the groups are not too bad. But if you know the rifle is sighted correctly and they keep missing, or if you are having trouble bringing a scope in to final zero, suspect a flinch.

Just don't let the shooters decide if that's the trouble. They always deny it.

It's easy to prove, though. Start loading the rifle for them one shot at a time. After you gain their confidence, pretend to load the gun, but do not. Hand them the empty rifle and watch when they shoot. If they are flinching, it will be very apparent and undeniable, even to the shooter.

It has to be a surprise, though. If they know the gun is not loaded, they will be as steady as an oak tree on a calm day.

How to deal with flinching is another thing altogether. But the one sure thing is that it's time to stop shooting for that day. It will only get worse.

Eating Scopes

I shoot a lot, and since familiarity breeds contempt, I sometimes need to be reminded again to respect hard-recoiling rifles.

Some time back, I was sighting in a few rifles, and because my buddy was using my rest and sandbag setup I moved to another bench and tried a slick plastic rest that was sent to me for evaluation. The weather was quite cold, and I was wearing a lot of loose-fitting winter clothing. I remember thinking before I pulled the trigger that the slippery plastic rest wouldn't provide any friction to hold the rifle and that I wasn't exactly sure where the butt was through all those layers of clothing.

Thank God it was a cold day and there weren't many people at the range, because it was embarrassing with all the blood pouring down the front of me. (The last time I did this was at the Outdoor Writers Association of America's annual shooting day, where I had an audience of hundreds who were undoubtedly impressed with the gun writer who was bleeding all over the new gun displays.)

Once again, I had a scope-shaped gash on the bridge of my nose that would certainly add to the collection of scar tissue there from past indiscretions. In any case, the lesson for today is that big guns kick, and if you become careless with that fact, they will remind you in a most unpleasant way, usually by feeding you the scope.

So please, "don't try this at home." Instead, let us gun writers do the experimenting for you and pass the lessons on; after all, it's our job. Keep in mind also that you too can avoid pain and embarrassment by remembering to mount and hold the gun properly. And watch the eye relief!

Big guns kick, and if you become careless with that fact, they will remind you in a most unpleasant way, usually by feeding you the scope.

to the front will transmit a lot less perceived recoil to the shooter's face. Also, choose a wide butt that is angled to fit snugly against the entire shoulder so that the recoil is distributed over as much surface as possible.

Synthetic stocks help to lessen the perceived recoil. It is thought that they will "flex" under recoil, acting like a big shock absorber. Certainly, many shooters report feeling much less recoil when using a synthetic stock.

High-tech recoil pads with highly engineered construction and materials, such as those sold by Uncle Mike's or Pachmayr, lessen what the shoulder feels. PAST Sporting Goods makes several shoulder protectors in vests or on a harness designed to be worn by the shooter that use similar recoil-absorbing materials. There are even models specifically for women.

MUZZLE BRAKES

Mag-Na-Port, KDF and other companies can add recoil-reducing muzzle brakes to a rifle, while just about every gun company today offers muzzle brakes on its factory guns. These brakes are amazingly effective at reducing felt recoil. However, they can be loud and so might not be advisable for hunting, when hearing protection is rarely worn. Some brakes, such as those made by Remington and Weatherby, are removable, so they can be used for practice and taken off for hunting. (Hunters don't feel the recoil when they are shooting at game; they are too focused to notice.) Just remember to check your rifle's zero without the brake because it can change when it is removed from the barrel.

Savage even makes a brake that you can turn on or off by twisting. The BOSS (Ballistic Optimizing Shooting System) found on Browning and Winchester guns can be replaced with a CR (Conventional Recoil) BOSS without the ports. It still provides the barrel-tuning ability of the BOSS, but without the noise or the recoil dampening. Both of these also keep a constant barrel dynamic so that accuracy or point of impact doesn't change like it can with removable brakes.

Noise and muzzle blast are as large a flinch-inducing problem as recoil, and a shooter should never fire a rifle with or without a brake, except in rare hunting situations, without hearing protection.

Banish all those recoil demons and practice with that new rifle. Your taxidermist will love you for it.

SCOPES

few hunters still cling to using iron sights on their rifles. That's fine, of course, and it's a personal choice, but the reasons given usually won't stand up to the light of examination. One I often hear from Eastern deer hunters is that iron sights are faster on running deer. Nothing could be further from the truth. In the hands of an experienced shooter, scopes are much faster and more accurate than any iron sights. Open sights require that three separate points of focus be dealt with: the rear sight, the front sight and the target. The human eye is not capable of focusing on all three, and to shoot well, you must keep the front sight in sharp focus.

Peep sights allow you to ignore the rear sight, but you still must focus on the front sight.

Other than the obvious problems this creates with trying to aim, it causes the target to "blur" out. That's fine if you are target shooting, but when you are hunting, it would be better to keep watch of the animal. You want it in sharp focus so that you can stay attuned to any body language or a change in position.

Scopes, on the other hand, magnify and brighten the image while putting the sights (crosshairs) on the same focal plane as the target, allowing both to stay sharp in your vision. A shooter with a low-power scope will always be a faster and more accurate field shot than the hunter who insists on using iron sights.

Only a couple of decades ago, another argument against scopes was that they were unreliable and prone to failure in poor weather. I remember that back in the early '70s, I had a pair of the old (pre-Blount) Weaver K-4 scopes mounted on the only two rifles I owned. The weather in Vermont's November deer season is consistent only in its inclemency, and it was never a question of if these scopes would fog up, but when. Every December for several years found me at the post office sending one or both of these scopes back to Texas for repairs.

Things have changed, though, and it's been a long time since I have seen an undamaged, quality scope fog up while hunting. (This includes the new Weavers, which are now good scopes for the money.) Junk is still junk, and you get what you pay for, but the quality of most scopes on the market is so much better today that fear of failure is no longer a viable reason to not use a scope.

EYE & EAR PROTECTION

his one is a no-brainer.

Simply put, if you fire even a single round at the shooting range without high-quality eye and ear protection, you are a total moron.

One simple question: How much hunting are you going to be doing when you are blind? I suppose you can still hunt if you are deaf, but it won't be fun, and your success will be less than sterling.

It takes about a millionth of a second to lose your sight, and you can't know when it's coming. Your gun or the gun of the guy next to you can blow up; it can potentially happen to any gun at any time. But the possibility of splashback

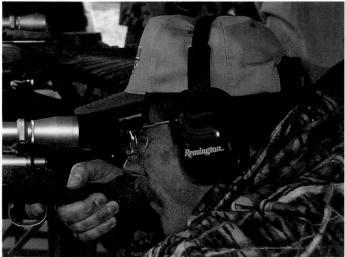

You're putting your sight and hearing at risk if you go to the range without good eye or ear protection. The rule is simple: Take the time to put on shooting glasses and ear muffs. Never bend or break this rule. Can the message be any clearer?

from the bullet is just as real. My cousin Philip can attest to that. He was hit in the leg by splashback and it penetrated through his new jeans and stopped when it hit his femur. Philip is a big, rugged guy with muscular legs, and if it penetrated to the bone in his thigh, it could certainly have taken out an eye with no problem.

Save your money to buy the best shooting glasses you can afford, and wear them every single time you fire a gun. No exceptions. That includes hunting.

Hearing loss is not immediate but is instead a cumulative effect. Every time you fire a gun without ear protection, you lose a little more hearing. If you don't think that can add up, ask an old shooter from your grandfather's generation, when

they rarely wore ear protection. But write your question down, because I doubt he will hear you. I have been lucky to meet several of the old gun writers whose work I had been reading for years. They all seemed to have the same limited vocabulary.

"Huh?"

"What?"

Admittedly, it's hard to wear hearing protection while hunting, although I wear my Walker's Game Ears more and more while big game hunting. They enhance my hearing as well as use suppression circuits to protect my ears from noise damage. If there are going to be multiple shots fired, such as when I'm waterfowl hunting or shooting varmints, I always wear them.

Walker's Game Ears—good hearing protection you can wear while hunting.

There are some guns I simply will not shoot without hearing protection. When I am hunting with my .454 Casull handgun, a pair of earplugs hangs from the shoulder holster. I don't care if it is a world-record buck—if he won't hang around long enough for me to put the plugs in my ears, he's as safe as a babe in its mother's arms. I am the same way with some of the big rifles I use that are equipped with muzzle brakes. Brakes are great for reducing recoil, but they increase the blast and noise considerably. I put in earplugs or take the brakes off the rifles. I don't shoot them, even hunting, without protection. I have in the past, but I won't again. My hearing is already bad from a variety of causes, including shooting. I intend to protect what's left.

Audiologists tell me that shooting "once in a while" while hunting should produce only minimal lasting damage. They caution, though, to always wear hearing protection when shooting at the range or any other place it's practical.

Furthermore, your shooting will be much better if you wear protection. A loud muzzle blast can contribute to flinching as much as recoil.

THE VALUE OF A FOULING SHOT

The first shot is always the most important when you are hunting, but if you are using a clean rifle, the bullet may not be headed for the spot you thought it was. The first shot from a clean rifle barrel rarely hits in the same place as those that follow it. That's the reason most target shooters fire a "fouling shot" before competing. This phenomenon can be even more pronounced if there is oil or solvent left in the bore of the rifle to protect it from rust.

With some rifles, it's hardly noticeable, and the first bullet hole will be almost in the group when firing multiple shots. Other rifles, though, can be vastly different. I had one .243 Win. that would not even hit the target at 100 yards if the barrel was clean and oiled. After that, it would settle down and shoot groups with bullet holes snuggled together like pigs in a pile. In fact, that rifle may well have been the most accurate sporter-weight gun I have ever owned. All except with the first shot.

Perhaps owning that rifle planted some deep psychological seed in my mind, but I don't like to hunt with a rifle that has a clean barrel. I usually shoot a fouling shot or two before going into the woods. If the rifle has gotten wet during the hunt, I usually just dry it out, wipe down the outside and shoot it to clean the water out of the bore. If I can't shoot and must clean a rifle during the hunt, I fire a fouling shot as soon as possible.

After testing hundreds of rifles at the range, I know that a fouling shot is not usually necessary. Unless you leave a lot of oil in the bore, most guns will hit close enough to the point of aim that you won't miss a big game animal. But firing a fouling shot makes me feel more confident. That alone can be important.

The best policy is to test your rifle with a clean and lightly oiled bore to see how it reacts.

Then play the odds and hunt with a fouled barrel!

All the shots you take at the range—save for one—are through a fouled barrel. That's how your gun was sighted in, that's how you conduct practice sessions. Field shooting conditions offer enough variables as it is. Why add a sparkling-clean barrel to the mix? Hunt with a fouled barrel and make that shot go where you expect it to.

The author recommends hunting with a fouled barrel—one through which at least one shot has been fired. A good time to do this is at your last sight-in session before the hunt. It makes better sense, and is a lot safer, than blasting a bullet into the ground at 5:30 a.m. before you head out into the field.

Chapter 6

ZERO OPTIONS

One day many years ago, my grandfather, his best friend and several other men were sighting in their rifles in preparation for the impending deer season. Gramp's friend had been shooting for a while, and they finally had his rifle hitting the paper target—but not much more—when the guy decided to quit.

"Hey, Buff," Gramp said. "That gun's nowhere near sighted in right; don't you think we ought to get it a little better before you go deer hunting?"

Never one to dote on the details, Buff answered with a casual wave of his hand, "Naw, it's close enough; they jump around a lot."

He meant the deer, of course, and his plan was to shoot and hope that one jumped in the direction of the bullet. Somehow, for him it always seemed to work, and he took his share of whitetails.

The rest of us would be better served to sight our hunting rifles in a little more carefully.

Time and again, I have been in camps with hunters who didn't bother to check the zero on their rifles. Some were proud of the fact, others argumentative. "It was fine last year, what can change?" they ask with barely concealed hostility.

More than one of these guys found out when he missed the chance of a lifetime. I could tell you I was gracious and didn't gloat in pointing out that I had told him he was making a mistake. But I'd be lying.

Sighting in your rifle before a big game hunt is as fundamentally important as buying a license. If you forget that or choose to ignore it, in my never-humble opinion, you deserve to miss.

THE CORRECT WAY TO
SIGHT IN A RIFLE

"nother miss; let's bore-sight that sucker again."
And so they did.

They took out the bolt, and while one held the rifle, the other looked through the bore and "adjusted" the scope. Defying all logic, the deer waited patiently in the field, where the hunter missed him another time or two before the buck decided he had an appointment somewhere else and boogied.

I just stood mute with amazement at the stupidity of it all. If there is anything more important to the preparation of

your hunt than properly sighting in your rifle, it escapes my notice. But so many hunters, either through ignorance or laziness, neglect to do it right. Why gamble on something so easily controlled?

STEP 1: A SOLID REST

The only way to sight in a rifle is to shoot from a solid rest. It's not a test of your shooting ability—it is an adjustment process for a precision instrument. You must eliminate all human error, and your skill—or lack of it—should not affect the outcome.

Use a shooting bench and sandbags or another rest that will support both the forearm of the rifle and the toe of the buttstock. This rest should be firm but with some "give." It has to hold the rifle perfectly still, and pillows or rolled-up blankets often fail to do that. They are too flexible and soft, and the rifle can move on them too easily. It will be difficult to hold the gun still against the forces of your body's functions, such as breathing or your heartbeat. At the same time, the support can't be hard, and it must be able to flex and move a little when the gun fires, or accuracy will be poor and your zero may not be correct for field shooting.

Sandbags are best; you can buy commercial bags or make your own. Commercial rests with dense foam between the gun and the rest are also good because the foam provides a solid, but flexible, rest. Regardless of what you use, you must support the forearm, never the barrel of the rifle. You must also support the toe of the stock near the butt. You will find that the front support must be higher than the rear. To achieve this, simply boost the front sandbag with a couple of boards, a cement block or whatever else is handy, as long as

Pad Your Shoulder: Just Do It!

*I*f the gun has any degree of recoil, it's a good idea to have a pad of some kind between the gun and your shoulder when you are ready to fire live ammo. Again, this is not a test of how tough you are and how much recoil you can absorb. There are some commercial pads on the market that are very good, but I often use an athletic elbow pad that I bought in a sporting goods store. Another thing that works well is a section of foam insulation made for water pipes. This not only has the foam to absorb recoil, but the hollow center acts like a shock absorber. These are inexpensive and can be found at any home supply store. If the gun is a large caliber, a small sandbag between you and the gun is a good idea.

The only way to sight in a rifle is to shoot from a solid rest. Sighting in is not a test of your shooting ability; it is an adjustment process for a precision instrument. You want to minimize any human error.

STEP 2: BORE SIGHTING

Your gun should be bore-sighted before you start. If you don't have access to an optical bore sighter, you can remove the bolt and settle the gun into your rest. Look through the bore at the target and center the bull's eye in the bore. Without moving the rifle, look through the scope and adjust the crosshairs until they are also centered on the bull's eye.

Since sandbags are made to support a rifle for shooting rather than for standing alone, one trick for holding the rifle still is to cut V-shaped wedges out of opposite sides in a cardboard box to hold the rifle. Put a little weight in the box and wedge the gun into the cuts to hold it still while you adjust the scope. Bore sighting will only get you on the target to allow you to finish sighting in by shooting. You should never consider hunting with a rifle that has been only bore sighted.

STEP 3: START CLOSE

Buy some decent targets designed for sighting in rifles; they are far better than anything homemade. What you pin them to is unimportant as long as it holds the target steady. I often just staple a target to a large cardboard box and throw a few blocks of wood in the box bottom to hold it down.

Put a target at 25 yards and carefully fire a shot at the center. You should be able to see the bullet hole through your scope. If you can't, mark it on the target with a piece of tape or a black marker so that you can. Lock your rifle into the sandbags and center the crosshairs on the bull's eye. Without moving the rifle, adjust the scope until the crosshairs move from the bull's eye and are centered on the bullet hole. You may wish to use the slotted cardboard box you made for this as well. Fire another shot at the center of the target. You should be pretty close to dead-on at 25 yards. If not, repeat the process.

STEP 4: MOVE OUT, DRY FIRE

Move the target to 100 yards and shoot from your sandbags or rest again, being careful to make sure the rifle is rock

Nothing's more important to the preparation of your hunt than properly sighting in your rifle. Why gamble on something so easily controlled and so essential to the sources of your hunt?

it's stable. The key is to try to keep the gun as low to the bench as possible.

The bench should be shaped so that there is a "wing" along your right side (for right-handed shooters). This allows you to support the rear of the rifle while your body is positioned correctly for shooting. Snug yourself into the bench so that your chest is pushing against it both in the front and on the side wing. This will wedge you into a "corner" and will make you more solid. The trick is to eliminate all movement.

Making Sandbags

One way to make sandbags is to recycle your old pants. Take an old pair of jeans, cut off one leg and shorten it to about 12 inches. Sew one end completely shut and sew the other end closed for all but 2 inches. Using the 2-inch hole, fill the bag 90 percent full of dry sand, then sew the hole shut.

Another good source of sandbags is the cloth bags used for shipping shot for reloading shotgun shells. Simply fill them with sand and sew shut.

steady and your scope is on its highest power. Do not try to hold the rifle as you would when hunting; placing your left hand under the forearm will induce movement. Instead, use your left hand to move and adjust the rear sandbag until the crosshairs are on the bull's eye. You should not be supporting the gun's weight at all; let the sandbags do that. The minute you try to hold the gun, you induce movement. The only reason you are touching the rifle is to pull the trigger and so that you can avoid being hit by the scope when the gun recoils.

At this point, you and the rifle should be rock steady and the crosshairs should not be moving. If they are, then you need to reevaluate your rest and your position at the bench until everything is stable. You should feel like you are "locked in" to the bench and the rifle, almost like you are all one piece.

With the gun empty, aim at the bull's eye and slowly squeeze the trigger until the gun dry-fires. (This will not hurt a modern centerfire rifle.) The crosshairs should not have wavered off the bull's eye. Continue to practice this dry-firing until you can do it every time without the crosshairs moving.

Step 5: Fire Groups, Make Adjustments

Being careful to squeeze the trigger slowly, fire a group of three shots. Find the center of the group and make your adjustments from there according to the instructions with your scope. If you lack the instructions, most American scopes move 1/4 inch per click at 100 yards. Be aware, though—some scopes are 1/2 inch and a few are 1/3 inch per click.

After making the scope adjustments, use the soft end of a bullet to gently tap on the scope's adjustment rings. Often, the internal adjustments will stick a little, and tapping on the scope will help to seat them. If you don't do this, the scope many not move until you fire the rifle again, so your next shot will not reflect the changes you made, which can be confusing.

If your target doesn't have grid lines, mark a cross with the intersection of the lines on the center of the bull's eye. Find the center of your three-shot group and measure straight over to the vertical line. This will give you the amount of left or

This hunter is sighting in the right way. Note: the butt end of rifle is supported, for more accuracy; recoil protection is present, to keep the shooter fresh and unflinching; eye and ear protectors are where they're supposed to be—on the eyes and ears.

right adjustment you need to make in the scope. Now measure up or down to the horizontal line and make the adjustment for that.

Allow the rifle to cool down a bit, and then fire three more carefully aimed shots. Your group should now be centered on the target. If for some reason it is not, repeat the process until it is. Always fire at least a three-shot group before making adjustments. If you fire one shot and adjust from that, you can spend all your time and ammo chasing bullet holes. A group will show if you are flinching or experiencing other shooting problems or if your rifle has accuracy problems; one shot will not.

Let the rifle cool off before firing your final group to see if there is a point-of-impact change from a hot barrel. Remember, you will always fire your first shot at big game from a cold barrel. Make certain that you adjust your final point of impact from the same cold barrel.

SIGHTING OPTIONS: HOW TO ZERO

W here to set your bullet's point of impact for a big game hunting rifle is subject to some discussion. However, I have found it is best to zero for a specific circumstance, determined by the game and terrain to be hunted.

THICK COVER

When hunting in thick woods, I zero my rifles dead-on at 100 yards. Assuming a scope height of 1.5 inches, the bullet path on most cartridges will stray little more than an inch from the line of sight from about 25 yards out to about 150 yards. It's not often that a shot in thick country is outside these parameters, and this intimacy between the line of sight and bullet path is most helpful when you must thread a bullet through a tiny hole in the brush. For longer shots, I simply know the bullet's drop and compensate as needed, although little is necessary out to 200 yards or more with most modern cartridges.

For this to work correctly, it is important to have the scope mounted as close to the bore as possible. High scope mounts such as "see-through" mounts, which position the scope higher so that the barrel-mounted iron sights can also be used, change the relationship between the line of sight and the bullet path too much. The result is that although you are seeing a clear path through the brush

ALWAYS Check Your Zero

Always check your rifle's zero after any kind of travel. This is particularly important after air travel because the vibration from airplanes can move a scope's adjustments. Also, airline baggage handlers seem to have a particular hatred for gun cases and will treat them like they were designed for the long toss or to be used as a ramp for their runway vehicles. This savagery can knock even the best scopes out of zero.

If there is no obvious damage to the rifle or the case, most of the time your gun will be shooting fine. But I can guarantee you that the one time you fail to check the rifle before hunting is the one time that your zero will be off. I know this from hard experience. Trust me; it's not worth missing the trophy you spent all that money and traveled all that way for because of something so easy to check.

It's a good idea to recheck the rifle's zero periodically during the hunt. This is even more important if the hunting includes a lot of

You may only get one shot, so make sure your rifle's zero is correct. This hunter is verifying that the sight on his rifle is adjusted properly.

time in vehicles or boats, where the engine's vibration can affect it. Also, keep an eye on the zero when hunting from horses. Horses have a nasty habit of banging your scabbard on trees when you aren't there to notice.

In fact, it's a bad idea to ever leave a rifle in a scabbard on a horse when you are not mounted. You may come back to find it in pieces. Check your zero every time you fall or bump the rifle hard. Also, weather or the simple process of hunting can change the zero on a rifle.

If you experience a dramatic change in point of impact, look for loose or broken screws, especially in the scope mounts. Also, check for bedding problems from a stock swelling or shrinking from wet or dry conditions. Another common field problem that can affect accuracy or point of impact is a cracked or split stock.

Remember, you may only get one shot; take the time now and then to make sure it will go where you want it to when that chance comes along.

---

to the target, the bullet path can be significantly different from your line of sight, and the bullet may impact a branch that is well above or below where you are looking.

OPEN COUNTRY

When hunting in more open country where a longer shot is a possibility, I prefer to sight dead-on at 200 yards. With most modern cartridges, this translates into about 2 inches high at 100 yards and about 8 inches low at 300 yards. Most of us have no business shooting at unwounded game beyond an honest 300 yards, so if you hold your crosshairs on deer hair (high above center, but never above the animal's back on the long shots) at any range you're attempting to shoot, you will take your game. Any time you put "air" instead of "hair" under the crosshairs, you induce guesswork that usually results in the bullet going someplace other than where you wanted it to. If the animal is that far away, use your hunting skills to get closer.

Regardless of the method of sighting you choose, do it well and be fussy about getting it right. You will be rewarded with a rifle that offers no surprises during the hunt.

High-velocity cartridges such as the .300 Winchester magnum will extend the practical range regardless of the sighting option selected.

The reality is that most shots will be 200 yards or less. If you sight for a point of impact that is farther than 200 yards, the mid-range trajectory (the high point of the bullet's arc) will be increased. Often, that apex, or high point, coincides with the range where the majority of big game animals are taken. Most hunters misjudge range by overestimating, and as a result, most misses on big game are high. It would be easy with a slight miscalculation in range or in shooting form to shoot over the animal, particularly if the trajectory arc has the bullet too high at that point to start

with. It's better to play the odds, which are that more of your shots will be less than 200 yards than will be past 200 yards. Keep your rifle's bullet trajectory so that you will have the least amount of guesswork with the most shots.

POINT-BLANK OPTION

The final popular method is to sight for a point-blank range. That is, to adjust the sights so that the bullet will not rise above or fall below a certain distance from the line of sight over a given range.

For example, for a 6-inch zone, the bullet will never be more than 3 inches above the line of sight during its trajectory arc. At some point the bullet will drop below the line of sight and continue to drop. Where it drops below the line of sight by 3 inches is considered the point-blank range. It helps to envision this as shooting through a pipe, in this case an 6-inch-diameter pipe. The line of sight is exactly down the center of the pipe, and the sights are adjusted so that the bullet's path will never rise higher than the top of the pipe or fall below the bottom edge of the pipe until it reaches the maximum point-blank range.

The theory behind this is that with a target zone of 6 inches (or whatever number you select), you can hold dead

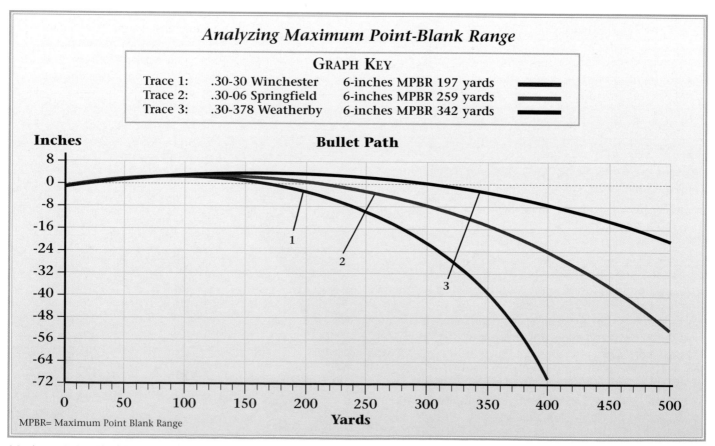

Maximum Point-Blank Range (MPBR) is the distance out to which you can hold your crosshairs or sights right on target, and achieve a hit. This graph depicts different MPBRs for different calibers, allowing for a 6-inch zone: 197 yards (1) for the .30-30, 259 yards (2) for the .30-06 and 342 yards (3) for the .30-378.

center on the animal and expect to hit the kill zone at any range out to the maximum point-blank range.

Of course, if you use this method, you should allow some compensation for the variables, such as shooter error, rifle accuracy, differences in animal size, wind, miscalculations in range, etc. If you are shooting at a deer with a 10-inch kill zone, it would be best to adjust the rifle for a 6-inch (never more than 3 inches above or 3 inches below the line of sight) point-blank range.

You can find information on point-blank range for various cartridge and bullet options in many ammo catalogs or reloading manuals. All the popular ballistic computer programs can figure the exact point-blank range for your rifle and load.

Regardless of the method of sighting you choose and what kind of "Zero" you strive for, make sure you. Do it well. Be fussy about getting it right, and memorize the rifle's trajectory until it is second nature to you when you shoot. Do all this and you will be rewarded with a rifle that offers no surprises during the hunt.

With this .270 Winchester sighted about two inches high at 100 yards it will be dead on at 200 yards and about 8 inches low at 300 yards. The scope should be adjusted to move the impact to the right about ¾ inch.

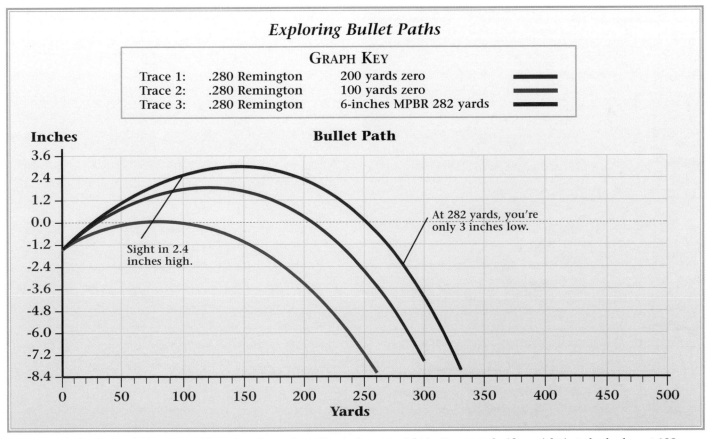

Exploring Bullet Paths

GRAPH KEY

Trace 1:	.280 Remington	200 yards zero	
Trace 2:	.280 Remington	100 yards zero	
Trace 3:	.280 Remington	6-inches MPBR 282 yards	

Bullet Path

Sight in 2.4 inches high.

At 282 yards, you're only 3 inches low.

Look at the bullet paths of this .280 and how they change depending on how you sight in. For example, if you sight in to be dead-on at 100 yards, you'll have to start holding high on game at a little over 200 yards. But sight in to be about 2.4 inches high at 100 yards, and you can hold right on your game's chest out to about 282 yards (MPBR with a 6-inch zone).

UNDERSTANDING TRAJECTORY

The law of gravity dictates that a bullet will begin to drop toward the earth from the moment it leaves the rifle barrel.

The reason that some rifles shoot "flatter" than others is simply because their bullets travel faster and are able to cover more distance in a given amount of time. The bullets still drop to the earth at a rate of acceleration of 32 fps, but they simply cover more ground than slower bullets before dropping a given distance.

It is necessary to elevate the rifle's bore slightly above the line of sight so that, when firing, the bullet's path rises on a curve that has it crossing the line of sight twice. Because the bullet begins dropping as soon as it is free from the constraints of the rifle, if it were simply fired with the bore of the rifle pointed at the target, it would hit below the target every time.

The line of sight is a straight line from the sights to the target. Vision is not subject to gravity, so your eye and the bullet take different paths to the target. While your eye's path is as straight as a laser, the bullet's path will be an arch to compensate for the effects of gravity.

THE BULLET'S PATH

The first time the bullet crosses your line of sight will be close to the rifle. The exact distance will depend on several factors, such as the height of the sights or scope above the bore, the distance to your zeroed point of impact and the relative flatness of the bullet's trajectory. However, this distance is usually somewhere around 25 to 50 yards. The next time the bullet crosses your line of sight will be at the distance you have selected to zero your rifle for. At any point in the bullet's path other than these two, the bullet will be above or below your line of sight.

Because a slower bullet takes longer to get to a given distant point, it must arch higher above the line of sight than a bullet that is traveling much faster. Let's take an extreme example and compare the .45-70 Gov. and the .300 Rem. Ultra Mag., both sighted for 200-yard zero (see graphs on page 126).

The mid-range trajectory is the apex of the bullet's arch, or the highest point that the bullet will be above the line of sight during its flight. With the .300 Rem. Ultra Mag. and a 200-yard zero, the mid-range trajectory of the bullet occurs at

Types Of Ballistics

The three common types of ballistics often referred to by shooters can be a little confusing. But it's really very simple.

Internal Ballistics. This is what happens inside the gun. It refers to the powder burning, pressure, the bullet's path down the barrel, etc.

External Ballistics. This is what happens during the bullet's flight through the air. It deals with trajectory, velocity, energy, etc.

Terminal Ballistics. This is what happens after the bullet has hit the target. It's the study of things such as expansion, weight retention, penetration, etc.

Look Out Below

Remember that your line of sight is different from the bullet's path. The bullet is traveling along a line that's somewhat lower than what you are seeing for the first several yards. The higher the scope is above the bore, the more pronounced this difference between the line of sight and bullet path becomes.

Make sure you have plenty of clearance for the bullet. It's easy to overlook a close obstacle, because you are concentrating on the distant target and not what's up close. Also, things that are close are usually blurry in the scope, or not even in the field of view.

The best illustration of this was when I was hunting prairie dogs in South Dakota with some buddies who I

Remember: Your line of sight is different than the bullet's path. That's well illustrated by the tight five-shot group on the hood of this truck.

suppose should remain nameless. I was sitting in a Jeep, spotting with binoculars for a shooter who had a sandbag on the hood of another vehicle. He shot five times, but I never saw a bullet strike. I do remember remarking to a friend sitting in the driver's seat of my Jeep that the rifle sounded funny. The ricochet sound was coming too soon after the shot.

The shooter finally gave up and in frustration said, "Bring your rifle over here and see if you can hit anything."

As I was preparing to shoot, I noticed a tight five-shot group on the hood of his rented Chevy Suburban. Every bullet kissed the far side of the hood before taking off into the wild blue yonder.

Comparing Bullet Path and Line of Sight

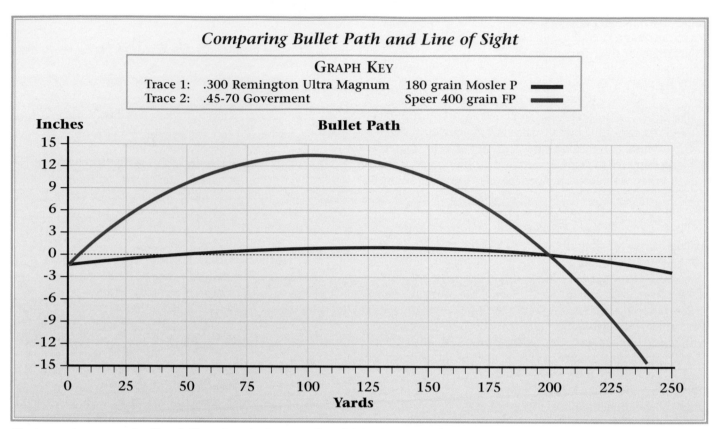

Here's an extreme example of how bullet path varies from your line of sight, depending on what caliber and cartridge you are using. The .45-70 Gov. here requires a rainbow-like trajectory to cross your line of sight at 200 yards. The .300 Rem. Ultra Mag. barely rises above your sight plane.

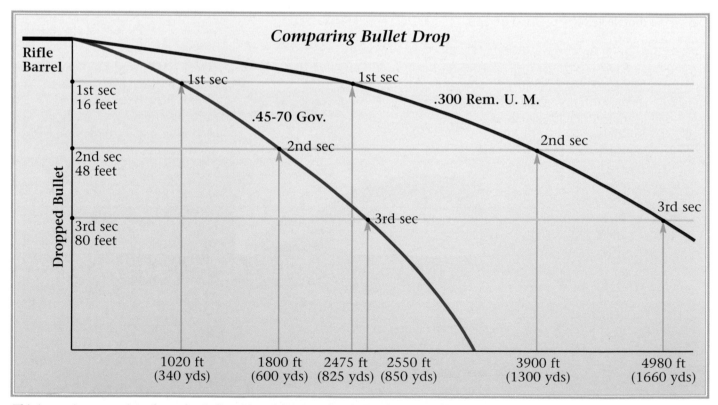

This interesting comparison shows that bullets dropped form your hand, shot form a .45-70 and shot from a .300 mag. all drop at the same rate. The difference is that the high-velocity .300 mag. bullet travels much faster … it gets farther out as gravity acts on it.

I remember participating in an industry-sponsored Western deer hunt some years ago. Present were some of the biggest names in the hunting business, and the combined hunting and shooting experience of the crowd was mind-boggling.

When we sighted in our rifles prior to the hunt, it was accepted without discussion that each rifle (all modern calibers) would be sighted 1.5 to 2 inches high at 100 yards.

The more I hunt in open places, the more I agree with this thinking. You can hold on out to 300 yards; if the shot's any farther ... get closer.

about 120 yards and is only 1.17 inches.

The mid-range trajectory for the .45-70 Gov. with a 400-grain bullet and a 200-yard zero is 13.37 inches and occurs at 110 yards.

Total bullet drop at 200 yards for the .300 Rem. Ultra Mag. is 6.99 inches. That is, if the bullet were fired perfectly level, it would have dropped 6.99 inches by the time it reached the 200-yard mark.

Total 200-yard drop for the .45-70 Gov. is 51.23 inches.

The difference is that the .300 Rem. Ultra Mag. has a muzzle velocity of 3,300 fps and uses a streamlined bullet. It takes the bullet only .19467 seconds in flight to reach 200 yards and the bullet is still traveling at 2,881 fps at that distance. The .45-70 Gov. uses a bullet that is much less streamlined, so it loses velocity much quicker and starts out at a much slower 1,300 fps. The .45-70 Gov. bullet crosses the 200-yard mark with a time in flight of .53846 seconds and with 991 fps of velocity remaining.

Simply put, any bullet must arch in its path to the target relative to the line of sight. The faster the bullet gets to the target, the flatter that arch or trajectory will be.

Chapter 7

BULLETS IN THE AIR

*I*t all changed the day that one of our hairy-legged ancestors picked up a rock and, instead of bashing his four-legged lunch fixin's in the head up close and dangerously personal, threw the rock to accomplish the same result from a safer distance. Since then, the hunting man has been trying to perfect the flight of deadly projectiles.

The path of today's modern hunting rifle bullet is invisible to most of us and a mystery. Yet it is an incredible feat when an accurate rifle is able to fire bullets with enough consistency that they can travel through the mass of assorted gases we call air and strike a predictable location, often a great distance from the shooter.

We have progressed a great deal from guns of the 1300s that fired almost anything that was handy, including rocks or gravel. Those crude handheld guns then were fired by inserting a glowing wire into a touchhole at the breech end or by using a glowing coal to light a small pile of powder on top of the touchhole. (Talk about long "lock time"!)

These guns were deemed the "devil's invention" by some clergy and were often outlawed for battle. (The crossbow met with a similar designation when Pope Innocent II forbade its use in 1139. He said crossbows were "deathly and hateful to God and unfit to be used among Christians." However, he noted that he didn't have a problem with skewering non-Christians with a longbow.)

At any rate, from these humble beginnings have evolved today's hunting rifles capable of firing hunting projectiles at 4,000 fps with accuracy that keeps all the bullets in less than 1 square inch at 200 hundred yards or more.

The witchery of it all remains, though, that during flight these bullets are out of our direct control and at the mercy of physics and fate.

That alone is enough to keep it interesting.

WHAT IS ACCURACY?

Just exactly what is accuracy, and how much of it can you expect from your rifle?

Accuracy is defined in the dictionary as the absence of error. In rifle shooting, the Speer #13 Reloading Manual defines it as the measure of precision in consistently obtaining a desired result. The accuracy of your rifle and ammunition is judged as the size of the group of bullet holes on a target when the rifle is fired from a stationary position. Groups are usually three or five shots, and because group sizes will vary, an average of several groups usually defines the rifle's accuracy ability.

This standard is usually judged at 100 yards, with the distance between the farthest-apart bullet holes measured from center to center.

WHAT'S ACCEPTABLE?

What can you expect from your rifle? Good question; every gun is different. However, out-of-the-box rifles should maintain a certain standard. Individual rifles have definite ammo preferences and will not shoot every load with equal accuracy. The following standards assume the best factory ammo for a given rifle, which may take some experimenting to find. These standards are for newer rifles, which shoot better than those made a generation ago.

The rifle should be well broken in with at least 100 rounds, preferably twice that many, through the bore with a proper break-in doctrine adhered to during that shooting. It also assumes that there are no mechanical problems with the rifle or sighting equipment. Finally, these are my standards and not everybody will agree with them.

It is my contention that under these conditions bolt actions and single-shots should put three-shot groups into 1.5 M.O.A. (minute of angle) or less. Pumps, lever actions and semiautos should shoot within two M.O.A. or smaller.

Admittedly, these standards are a little on the tough side. But I see no reason to accept anything less from today's rifles.

M.O.A. (Minute of Angle)

Rifle groups are often expressed in minute of angle, but what does that mean?

There are 360 degrees of angle in a full circle, and 60 minutes of angle in each degree. One minute of angle equals 1.047 inches per 100 yards. So, for practical purposes, one minute of angle equals 1 inch at 100 yards, 2 inches at 200 yards, 3 inches at 300 yards and so forth.

❧ ❧ ❧ ❧ ❧

ANGLE

One of the most confusing aspects of long-range shooting is what happens to the bullet's path when the shot is fired at a sharp uphill or downhill angle. I think I have heard every theory on earth, but the most common is that when you are shooting downhill, the bullet will strike higher, and when you are shooting uphill, the bullet will strike lower. Technically, both are wrong.

Gravity doesn't care if the bullet is flying up or down; it works its magic on it in exactly the same way. That is, if we disregard air friction, gravity pulls the bullet toward the center of the earth at a rate of acceleration of 32 fps. So when one second passes, the bullet is falling at 32 fps, and when two seconds pass, the bullet is falling at 64 fps, and so on.

GRAVITY IS THE KEY

Gravity is what causes a trajectory curve in every bullet fired. If we could fire a bullet in space, where there is no gravity, the bullet would not drop a bit. But here on earth, gravity is a fact of life. Gravity pulls on the bullet as it travels in relation to the center of the gravitational force, or the center of the earth. The longer gravity has to work on the bullet, the faster the bullet will drop.

Gravity doesn't care if the bullet is flying up or down. It works its magic on it in exactly the same way.

You must understand how a steep shooting angle can affect point of impact. If you don't, you could well miss the trophy of a lifetime.

The distance a bullet travels in relation to the earth's center (gravitational pull) from the muzzle to the target is what determines how far a bullet will drop. With a steep up or down angle, the distance to the target will be longer than the distance the bullet travels in relation to the earth's center. Rather than dropping the amount we expect for the distance traveled to the target, the bullet actually will drop for the distance it travels in relation to the earth's center. The steeper the angle, the shorter that distance becomes.

ONE EXAMPLE

For example, let's assume that you are shooting at a deer that is 400 actual yards away, but on a very steep angle, and you are using a 7mm Rem. Mag. with 140-grain factory loads, sighted for a 200-yard zero. You will expect the bullet to impact 18 inches below the line of sight for a 400-yard shot. However, the path of the bullet's flight in relation to the earth's center, or the center of gravitational pull, is in reality 300 yards, so the bullet is only 6 inches below the line of sight when it gets to the deer. If you hold for 400 yards, it will result in shooting over the ram you just paid $10,000 to hunt.

Of course, as the distance shortens, this becomes less of a factor because the bullet is moving faster and has less time in flight for gravity to act on it. The result is that, because of

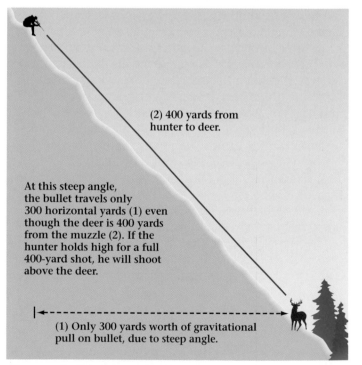

(2) 400 yards from hunter to deer.

At this steep angle, the bullet travels only 300 horizontal yards (1) even though the deer is 400 yards from the muzzle (2). If the hunter holds high for a full 400-yard shot, he will shoot above the deer.

(1) Only 300 yards worth of gravitational pull on bullet, due to steep angle.

The general rule is: Don't overcompensate for distance to your target when the angle is steep (either up or down) because your bullet will not drop as much as you would otherwise expect.

the shorter range, the bullet has dropped less and the trajectory curve is much flatter. Obviously, the flatter the rifle shoots, the less the difference will be. With a flat-shooting modern rifle and a sight-in that keeps the bullet within 3 inches of the line of sight out to a given distance, if the target is less than that distance from you, the bullet will always strike within 3 inches of your point of aim, regardless of the angle. This should not cause you to miss a big-game animal.

LONG SHOTS, STEEP ANGLES

The problem comes when you cannot close the distance and must take a long shot, compounded by an angle that's steep. Suppose the angle is very steep and the distance to the sheep is 300 yards, while the distance in relation to gravitational pull is 200 yards. With that same 7mm rifle, you will be expecting the bullet to drop 6 inches from the line of sight for a 300-yard shot, when in reality it will hit right where the crosshairs are centered because the rifle is zeroed at 200 yards, which is the actual bullet travel in relation to gravitational pull. With luck, if you held for a 6-inch bullet drop, you might spine the sheep instead of shooting over his back.

But the reality is that you are likely to miss this sheep as well because of another, and perhaps more important, factor. The steep angle causes you to view the sheep from a different perspective than how we are used to seeing animals. While in our minds we are seeing a broadside profile, the reality is that if the angle is down, you are looking at a lot of the sheep's back; if the angle is up, his belly. If you hold in the center, as

The solution to shots at steep angles is to use a very flat-shooting rifle and to try to keep your shots to a reasonable range.

you would for most shots, the crosshairs are likely on the intersection of his side and back (for the down shot). Because of the angle, a bullet that strikes even slightly higher than you expected will go over the sheep and once again ... miss.

The solution to shots at steep angles is to use a very flat-shooting rifle, try to keep your shots to a reasonable range and always force yourself to aim a little lower than you think you should to compensate for the viewing angle.

	Analyzing Bullet Drop at Various Angles		
	Angle (in degrees)	Bullet Path Below Line of Sight at 400 Yards (in inches)	Variance in the Bullet Path from Level (in inches)
	0 (level)	-23.14	NA
	10	-22.47	0.67
	20	-20.46	2.68
	30	-17.16	5.98
	40	-12.69	10.45
	50	-7.20	15.94
	60	-0.81	22.33

BRUSH GUNS

No single topic has remained so arguable over the decades as the issue of "brush guns." Advances in technology and trends of market whimsy have done nothing to stifle the discourse about which rifle "bucks the brush" better. Hunters of the old school say that a heavy, fat, blunt-nosed bullet traveling at low to moderate velocity will plow through brush with less deflection. The "enlightened" modern thinkers say that the long, thin bullet with a high rate of rotational speed will perform better because the gyroscopic effect of the rotation will keep it on course or aid it in returning to a stable course after a disturbance.

Then there is the matter of bullet construction. Certainly, a low-velocity bullet will need to be of a softer construction than a premium bullet designed for magnum-type impact velocities. It follows that the softer bullet will deform more easily than the tougher "modern" bullet and destabilize in flight. That is certainly true if the velocities are the same, but the very natures of the bullets dictate that the tougher bullet will be traveling at a higher velocity. What effect will that create?

Finally, there is the argument that in a given caliber, a round-nosed or flat-nosed bullet is better for shooting through brush than a pointed bullet. Nobody seems to know why, but a lot of hunters will argue the point passionately.

I have heard arguments on the extremes of both sides. A Saskatchewan outfitter once told me that his .35 Whelen would mow down the thick second-growth brush that domi-

nates the east side of the province like a "weed whacker through your front lawn." On the other hand, a manufacturer of a gun-related product told me during a SHOT Show dinner that if a bullet traveling over 3,500 fps even comes close to a tree branch, without necessarily hitting it, the pneumatic pressure of the air displaced by the bullet compressing against the tree branch will cause the bullet to fly off course and often even disintegrate in flight.

So who can you believe?

TESTING THE THEORY

I think that it is accepted that any bullet will deflect in flight if it hits brush. My grandfather's response to this was, "If you can see the deer well enough to shoot at it, then there is a hole big enough to fit a bullet through without hitting the brush." Good advice, but it still doesn't answer the question of bullet deflection.

To find out for myself, I decided to shoot several rifles through brush under controlled conditions and record the results. Because using actual brush provided inconsistent results, I turned to hardwood dowels to simulate brush.

I drilled holes in a couple of two-by-fours to hold the 1-foot dowels. The holes were carefully spaced with ⅛ inch between them to ensure that no bullet could slip between without hitting something.

Because the target backstop on our range is higher than the bench inside the shooting house, I constructed a frame to hold the "brush" high enough to approximately center the

groups on the plywood backstop. A target was hung between cross-members on the front of the frame. This was placed at a measured 10 yards in front of the backstop, which was 100 yards from the shooting house. One foot behind the target was a barrier of ⅜-inch dowels. Two feet behind that was another barrier of ¼-inch dowels. This was designed to be about twice as wide as the front barrier so that it would catch any deflected bullets.

I covered the backstop with white paper, and shooters fired three shots at the target with each gun without the "brush" in place to establish a center of impact on the backstop. Unless noted, we then fired five shots through the "brush" from each rifle. After each shot, we replaced the dowels and marked the resulting hit on the backstop. This ensured consistency in the "brush" encountered by all bullets.

All shots were fired from a benchrest, and caution was taken to make sure that they were carefully aimed. However, since I was recording the differences in group sizes before and after hitting the brush and the deviation from the center of impact, exacting accuracy was not necessarily important. All rifles showed acceptable hunting accuracy with the ammo selected, but the results are not to be interpreted as the "best" that rifle can shoot.

ANALYZING RESULTS

The results are recorded in the accompanying chart, but I will note some key points. Long, pointed bullets tended to keyhole (turn sideways), particularly when they hit the first

This .44 Mag. hit clearly illustrates the tendency of blunt bullets to "drill through" the brush. In contrast, the sleek pointed bullets would start to tumble when hitting a glancing blow on a dowel.

Many of the bullets keyholed after hitting the first barrier. Here the profile of a 100 gr. .243 bullet is clearly shown in the second barrier.

Testing For "Brush" Guns

Gun and Load	Extreme Spread of Group Before Brush (in inches)	Extreme Spread of Group 10 Yards After (in inches)	Percent of Increase in Group Size	Average from Group Center (in inches)	Farthest from Group Center (in inches)
.280 Rem. 140-grain Winchester	3	7	233	3.7	6.5
Comments: Shrapnel noted on second barrier. All bullets showed indications of tumbling, most after first barrier.					
.30-30 170-grain Winchester	5	12.25 (6.5 if you discount shot #3 which hit 2x4)	245 (30 without shot #3)	3.7 (2 without shot #3)	10 for shot 3; others, 4
Comments: Shot #3 hit a glancing blow on two-by-four and opened group. All hits showed indications of tumbling. Excellent performance if shot #3 is discounted.					
.220 Swift 50-grain Remington	2.25	11.75	522	4.3	7.25
Comments: All shots showed indications of tumbling, with four clear keyholes. Bullets appeared to stay intact.					
.35 Rem. 200-grain Winchester	3	4	33	1.75	3
Comments: No keyholes, but holes were ragged, indicating expansion or destabilization. Only one hit cleanly cut off a ⅜-inch dowel, all others "drilled" through between dowels. Best performance overall.					
.243 Win. 100-grain Winchester	2.5	16.25	650	6.65	8.75
Comments: All hits indicated tumbling. Shot #4 showed a perfect key in second barrier.					
.44 Rem. Mag. 240-grain Winchester	4.6	10.25 (4.6 without shot #1)	223 (Without shot group is the same size)	3 (1.75 shot #1)	(8 for shot #1) (2.75 without shot #1)
Comments: Without the flyer of shot #1, this is the best performance of all guns tested in terms of "after brush" group size and stability.					
.45-70 Gov. 400-grain handload	3	5	66	1.85	2.75
Comments: Some evidence of expansion or slight tipping on shots #2 and #4.					
.45-70 Gov. 300-grain Winchester	4.5	6.5	44	2.25	3.25
Comments: Shots #3 and #5 were enlarged, indicating expansion; shot #2 was smeared on side, indicating either expansion or destabilization.					

These are all the calibers tested as "brush" guns, except the .300 Savage. Left to right, .220 Swift, .243 Win., .270 Win., .280 Rem., 7 mm Rem. Mag., .30-30 Win., .308 Win., .30-06, .35 Rem., .35 Whelen, .44 Mag. and .45-70.

Gun and Load	Extreme Spread of Group Before Brush (in inches)	Extreme Spread of Group 10 Yards After (in inches)	Percent of Increase in Group Size	Average from Group Center (in inches)	Farthest from Group Center (in inches)

Testing For "Brush" Guns (continued)

Gun and Load	Extreme Spread of Group Before Brush (in inches)	Extreme Spread of Group 10 Yards After (in inches)	Percent of Increase in Group Size	Average from Group Center (in inches)	Farthest from Group Center (in inches)
.270 Win. 130-grain Winchester	2.25	10.25 (2.25 without shot #4)	456 (without #4, group is same size)	3.65 (3.06 without shot #4)	6
Comments: Shots #1, 2, 3 and 5 are in a 2.25 inch group that is 3.5 inches from impact center. Shot #4 is 9.5 inches from the center of that group and 6 inches from impact center.					
.30-06 165-grain Winchester.	2.25	8.25	366	3.3	4.5
Comments: All shots showed evidence of keyholing.					
.35 Whelen 250-grain Remington	1.9	6.75	355	2.35	3.5
Comments: All shots showed round or keyed holes, indicating tumbling.					
7mm Rem. Mag. 160-grain Winchester	2	11.5	575	3.5	6.5
Comments: All shots tumbled after the first barrier; all but one cut off at least two dowels in second barrier.					
.308 Win. 150-grain Winchester (shooter #1)	6.25	5.25	-19	2.9	3.75
Comments: Smaller group size after hitting brush made this unusual. All bullets showed indications of tumbling. Refired with different shooter to test again.					
.308 Win. 150-grain Winchester (shooter #2)	2.12	11	519	4.25	7.75
Comments: All shots keyholed on target.					
.300 Sav. 180-grain round nose	2.3	10.5	457	4.15	5.5
Comments: All bullets tumbled.					
.300 Sav. 150-grain pointed	6	14	233	7.45	8
Comments: Group size without shot #5 is 4.75 inches, located 8 inches below impact center. Shot #5 was 6 inches high. Bullets showed tumbling.					

dowels a glancing blow that put them between two dowels. Often, the second barrier would have two or even three dowels cut off, indicating that the bullet was traveling sideways.

Round- or flat-nosed bullets tended to track better and showed less tendency to keyhole. The old-timers who liked big, slow bullets were on to something. The .35 Rem., .44 Rem. Mag. (discounting one flyer) and .45-70 Gov. showed the lowest percentage change in group size.

To spoil the theory, the .270 Win. showed no change in group size if you discount the one flyer.

Check out the .308 Win.! It actually showed a smaller group after hitting the brush. All calibers showed evidence of losing stability or deforming.

In summary, you would be ill-advised to intentionally take any shot through brush at a deer. Every bullet that hits brush, regardless of caliber or design, will be affected, and it is impossible to predict reliably what that effect will be. While one caliber may do "better" than another, they all had the potential for extreme flyers. If that flyer happens to be the shot you fired at a buck, the results could be disastrous. Nothing's worse than making a poor hit on a magnificent game animal.

LONG-RANGE HUNTING RIFLES

This wasn't going quite like I'd planned.

Dark was becoming more than just a hint, and with its arrival, my deer hunting for another year would end, apparently with yet another unfilled tag.

I couldn't have been more ready as I sat in that Alabama shooting house. My rifle was a Weatherby Accumark, one of the best long-range factory guns ever built. Better still, it was chambered for the new .30-378 Wthby Mag., probably the flattest-shooting big-game factory cartridge ever designed. I had it scoped with a Leupold Vari-X III 6.5-20X50-30mm, and nestled in the rifle's chamber was a carefully crafted handload that would group its premium bullets so tight you would think they were in love. I knew the trajectory as well as I know my wife and had practiced enough with the rifle that the wife was getting jealous. A laser rangefinder had told me that I could see 685 yards to my left and 367 yards to the right, and I had landmarks at intervals in between, so I would know within a few yards how far any visible deer would be from me.

I was ready, all right, but for what? No deer wanted to come out and play with me.

Then the binoculars caught a movement back in the woods. I stared at the spot, but as the light faded even more, my heart kept sinking.

Then I saw movement again, and it had metamorphosed into a flicking ear. As I eased the Weatherby into shooting position, the buck stepped into the field. The crosshairs settled. I tickled the trigger, and when the big gun quit roaring,
the buck was lying as still as a tomb on top of the tracks he had just been occupying.

NOT JUST FOR TEXAS

The era of long-range deer rifles is upon us, and while some may argue that technology is replacing hunting, it is undeniable that hunters drive the market, and the market wants these guns.

With gun names like Sendero and Laredo, the deer hunter might conclude that these rifles are only for hunting in South Texas, but it "ain't necessarily so." In fact, the roots of these rifles can probably be traced to the Southeast. The early "bean-field" rifles created for hunting the large soybean fields of the region were the prototypes of what would evolve into this class of rifle. Designed for the hunter who prowled the huge agricultural fields of the area, they are engineered to be the ultimate in long-range rifles for deer-class big game.

Hunters everywhere are discovering that these rifles open up a new world of possibilities. They are seeing use in places as diverse as the open prairies of the central states to the planted, green fields of the Deep South. Eastern hunters are using them as they watch powerlines, and any place agriculture is an industry (and rifles are legal), these guns are shooting deer at barrel-stretching distances.

You must practice a great deal to reach a level of competence that allows you to take advantage of these guns. My reluctance in writing this is that it may encourage some to

Rifles—Some Long-Range Combinations				
Rifle	Ammo	Average Group Size (in inches)	Velocity (in fps)	Comments
Remington Model 700 Sendero SF	Winchester 220-gr. Silvertip	2.93	2,768	Good velocity but poor accuracy
Remington Model 700 Sendero SF	Remington 190-gr. ER BT	1.3	2,863	Good long-range deer load
Remington Model 700 Sendero SF	Federal 150-gr. Trophy Bonded	2.03	3,322	Poor accuracy
Remington Model 700 Sendero SF	Hornady 150-gr. Interlock	0.6	3,102	Best load tested
Rifle Averages		**1.71**	**3,013**	**Best velocity of rifles tested**
Savage 110 FP Tactical Rifle	Winchester 220-gr. Silvertip	1.1	2,663	Good accuracy
Savage 110 FP Tactical Rifle	Remington 190-gr. ER BT	.87	2,809	Good long-range deer load for this rifle
Savage 110 FP Tactical Rifle	Federal 150-gr. Trophy Bonded	2.47	3,188	Poor accuracy
Savage 110 FP Tactical Rifle	Hornady 150-gr. InterLock	0.78	3,077	Best load in this rifle
Rifle Averages		**1.3**	**2,934**	**Excellent accuracy and velocity**
Winchester Model 70 Classic Laredo BOSS	Winchester 220-gr. Silvertip	1.27	2,537	Better for bigger game than deer
Winchester Model 70 Classic Laredo BOSS	Remington 190-gr. ER BT	1.77	2,770	Erratic in this rifle
Winchester Model 70 Classic Laredo BOSS	Federal 150-gr. Trophy Bonded	1.46	3,236	Except for shot #2, shot acceptably well, best game bullet tested
Winchester Model 70 Classic Laredo BOSS	Hornady 150-gr. Interlock	0.6	3,2023	Best-shooting ammo at this BOSS setting
Rifle Averages		**1.27**	**2,891**	**Best average accuracy**

All are three-shot groups at 100 yards.
Velocities were measured 15 feet from the muzzle with an Oehler 35P chronograph.
All rifles in .300 Win. Mag.

Here are the results of accuracy tests using three good long-range rifles and a variety of cartridges.

think they can blast away at distant deer in hopes that their new gun and fancy scope will make up for a lack of ability. I hope that will not happen, but I am not so naive as to believe it won't. Slob hunters are slob hunters, no matter what they are shooting.

However, the hunter who practices and learns about long-range shooting will find that these rifles can extend their effective range considerably. The "effective range" is the distance that you can keep all your shots in a 6-inch circle under field conditions. (Six inches allows a margin of error for uncontrollable factors.)

THE RIFLES

Most long-range deer guns are essentially "varmint" rifles chambered for bigger calibers. They are not designed for the hunter on the move and are a poor choice for tracking a buck through the swamps of Maine. Instead, they are made

These are all excellent long-range deer cartridges. Left to right: .270 Weatherby Magnum, 7mm Remington Magnum, 7mm Weatherby Magnum, 7mm STW, .300 Winchester Magnum, .300 Weatherby Magnum and .30-378 Weatherby.

to be used from a fixed position while hunting from some sort of stand and usually shooting with the rifle supported by a rest of some kind. They do, however, need to be light enough to be carried for reasonable distances both while traveling to and from stands and in the event that a deer is hit and must be tracked.

Most hunters prefer these rifles chambered for one of the magnum cartridges: A .300 Win. Mag., 7mm Rem. Mag., .300 Wthby and the like.

At first glance, using these guns on deer would seem like napalming prairie dogs. But with today's excellent bullets, that's not really the case at all. By using a premium bullet, such as the 200-grain Nosler I used on that Alabama buck, meat damage is no worse than with other rifles. The key is in the very flat bullet trajectories these guns produce. The .30-378 Wthby Mag. has the flattest trajectory available from a factory rifle. When it's sighted for 300 yards, it is only 3.23 inches high at 150 yards and 7.41 inches low at 400 yards.

Remember, it's flat trajectories we are looking for here, because the flatter the trajectory, the better the odds are of hitting a long-range target. Flat trajectories require fast velocities, and high energy is a by-product. There is no such thing as "too dead," so too much energy is not a real problem if quality bullets are used.

With some of the standard calibers, the energy levels are really getting low at extended ranges. For example, the .25-06 Rem. drops below the long-accepted minimum

for deer of 1,000 fp at just past 400 yards. The .30-378 Wthby Mag. still has 2,865 fp at that distance, more than the .25-06 Rem. had at the muzzle. If killing game at long range is the goal, it's no contest.

The barrels are long to maximize velocities, with lengths of 24 to 26 inches standard, and they are almost always heavy contour and often fluted. As a rule, a heavy barrel will be more accurate than a light tube, simply because it vibrates less with the shot, and accuracy is the underlying principle in designing these rifles.

BULLET ADVICE

When it comes to bullets in these guns, there are a couple of things to keep in mind. First, you want the highest ballistic coefficient available within the weight you have chosen to keep trajectories flat. Perhaps more important, though, is that the bullet must be constructed to handle the impact velocities of these very fast cartridges. Some game will still be taken at relatively close range, and you will need to choose a bullet that will not come apart with the high-impact velocities of the close shots yet will still expand at the much lower velocities of long-range shots. That pretty much limits you to the "super premium bullets."

Oh, I almost forgot. That buck in Alabama? After I shot him, I measured the distance with the rangefinder.

Eighty-two yards.

Go figure.

The era of long-range deer rifles is upon us, and while some may argue that technology is replacing hunting, it is undeniable that hunters drive the market and the market wants these guns.

LONG-RANGE OPTICS

*L*ong-range precision big-game shooting is demanding. No other field of big-game hunting asks so much from the optics used because the distances are long and the targets are relatively small.

You get what you pay for in optics, and the best high-power rifle scopes are going to be expensive. It's a rare rifle scope that will provide the extreme magnification needed at long range and still have the clarity and resolution to see clearly. Inexpensive scopes will often "blur out" as the power increases. They also lack the solid mechanics needed to stand up to the severe recoil of big cartridges and to ensure that point of impact will not change as the scope is zoomed in or out. They also do not have adjustments that are sure, reliable and repeatable. In addition to rugged construction, top-quality optical glass is important, as is excellence in the coatings.

Why buy a super-accurate, long-range rifle and then choke up its performance with a junk scope? Good optics are expensive, but for a serious shooter they are as important and necessary as an accurate rifle.

No hunter I have ever met said he wishes he had bought cheaper optics. I have, however, known a lot who complained bitterly about the inexpensive scopes they were using.

Rangefinders

*T*here have been attempts for years to find a practical, portable way for hunters to judge range in the field, mostly with poor results.

A lot of those rangefinders were in scopes and were difficult to use. They depended on striation wires or mill-dots and comparing them in one way or another to the mythical "average" animal size. They were slow to use and often required complicated mathematical calculations. Accuracy was mediocre at best.

With the advent of affordable and portable laser rangefinders, these scopes are really obsolete for big-game hunting. This technology is changing so fast that it's hard to keep up, and anything I write about here will likely be surpassed by the time you read it. The newest rangefinders are small enough to fit in a coat pocket, easy to use and accurate to far beyond any distance we should be shooting rifles at game.

You simply point the unit, push a button and read the range. The readout is instantaneous and doesn't require that you mentally calculate mathematical equations that would make Stephen Hawking scream in frustration.

The price is low enough that anybody who wants one can afford it. Every rifle hunter who shoots beyond 200 yards should consider buying one.

With the advent of affordable and portable laser rangefinders, everything changed. For the first time we can judge our shooting range accurately and quickly.

BOSS

No area of rifle shooting has been more explored, caused more frustration and employed more gun writers than the quest for accuracy.

It has never been a secret that individual rifles can be fussy about what loads they like. There may not necessarily be anything wrong with the load itself—in other rifles, it may produce tiny groups—but in that rifle, it is simply incompatible.

It is a frustrating experience for a hunter to have decided on a specific factory load, only to discover that his or her rifle will not shoot it well. The hunter is left to either choose something different or live with the inaccuracy. Neither is a valid solution.

Any time a bullet is fired through a rifle barrel, it sets up a series of vibrations, not entirely unlike a water hose that whips around if it is not held, only to a lesser degree. Often, accuracy problems with specific loads can be traced to the timing of those vibrations. If the vibrations are consistent with accuracy when the bullet leaves the barrel, with all else constant, the rifle will shoot that load well. Sometimes, though, the vibrations are in a place that is not conducive to accuracy when the bullet exits, and a load that may actually be quite good will not shoot well in that particular rifle.

Armed with that knowledge, Browning developed a system that allows fine-tuning the length and, in turn, the vibrations of a barrel. They call it the BOSS.

BOSS is an acronym for Ballistic Optimizing Shooting System. It is, in essence, a weight threaded onto the end of the barrel and inscribed with a micrometer-type adjustment scale. By turning the weight and moving it in or out on

threads, you can effectively "tune" the barrel's vibrations to each load. The micrometer scale allows you to read the location of each setting and to judge how much change each movement creates.

This, of course, will not compensate for poor loads, bullets or shooting, but with those being what they should be, you can bring any quality load around to shoot pretty well in a BOSS-equipped rifle.

I first tested it in a .270 Win. fitted with a Burris 3X9 Signature series scope. After sighting in the rifle, I allowed it to cool, and then, using Federal 150-grain round-nosed ammo, I fired five-shot groups at different settings.

It was a thing of wonder to be able to dial changes in my group sizes. The first group was at the suggested setting of 6.0 and measured 1¾ inches. The next was at 7.0 and measured 1⅝ inches. I then turned it down to 5.0, and the group shrunk to ⅞ inch. When set at 4.0, the group opened up to 2 inches. If I were planning to hunt with this load, I would fine-tune by changing in small increments from the 5.0 setting until I found the absolute best setting.

As with most things, there is no free lunch. The BOSS eats up a little barrel length, and there is a corresponding drop in expected velocities. Also, most shooters agree that aesthetically, it's just plain ugly. Muzzle blast and noise are increased with the original recoil-compensating BOSS, but that can be corrected with the purchase of the CR (Conventional Recoil) BOSS, which is nonported. It won't reduce recoil, but it will tune the barrel's harmonic vibrations the same as the original BOSS.

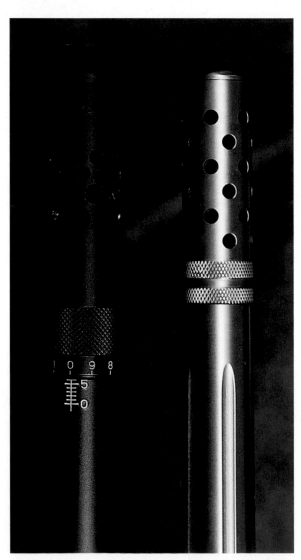

The barrel on the right is equipped with a Browning BOSS.

SHOOTING IN WIND

*T*he wind's effect on a bullet's flight has been a subject of heated discourse for as long as shooters have been trying to hit targets at long distances. We have developed charts and computer programs in attempts to make predictions, but at best, they are only a guideline. All the mathematical theorists from Einstein to my cousin Philip can't predict exactly what a bullet will do when it is fired through a real-world moving air mass.

However, the computer programs and ballistic tables are useful in teaching you the wind's effects, and it is hardly a waste of time to study them. For example, the accompanying table will give you some idea of the difference of wind direction on a bullet's path. It will also help to illustrate the degree of wind deflection on differing bullets and velocities. But the flaw in these tables and programs is that the predictions are built on laboratory conditions and assume a constant force and direction of wind.

LOOKING AT REAL-WORLD VARIABLES

Things are different in the atmosphere we shoot through. Winds gust and wane with currents and flows affected by terrain, vegetation and a million other factors. While it may be blowing one speed where you are, your bullet can travel through wind that is moving several different speeds before it reaches a distant target. The same goes with wind direction-over a given distance it can curl around, double back, eddy, switch and change its attitude more times than a six-year-old with a sugar buzz. If there is one constant in a wind's influence on a bullet, it is the inconsistency.

The effect, as predicted in the charts and computer programs, is based on the velocity and ballistic coefficient of the bullet, which determines the time of flight, or the amount of time the wind has to act on the bullet. The more time in flight, the more the wind will blow it off course. Other factors include the bullet's size and shape, which dictate the amount of area available for the wind to blow against. The bullet's weight is also important because it is easier to push around a light object than it is a heavy one. Whom would you rather wrestle, Hulk Hogan or Bill Gates? Same principle.

Wind direction is yet another factor. A 90-degree side wind will blow against the full profile of the bullet, but any angle that is different will be acting on a differing percentage of the bullet's surface. A full head or tail wind will have either the point or the base of the bullet to blow against, which affects retained velocity and, consequently, bullet drop. For example, a .44 Rem. Mag. 240-grain bullet with a 20 mph tailwind will have almost 100 fps more retained velocity at 500 yards than the same bullet with a 20 mph headwind. This will change the bullet path even though there is no theoretical wind drift and the difference in drop is almost 45 inches. Of course, this is an extreme example, and nobody really considers the .44 Rem. Mag. a 500-yard cartridge, but every bullet from any cartridge will be affected in some way.

Now suppose the wind is gusting from a 45-degree angle, or 20 degrees or perhaps 10 degrees. Maybe it will be from all three before the bullet makes it from your gun to the target.

Analyzing Wind Drift				
Cartridge/ Muzzle Velocity	Distance (in yards)	Drop/Drift in inches, with 20-mph wind from 6 o'clock	Drop/Drift in inches, with 20-mph wind from 3 or 9 o'clock	Drop/Drift in inches with 20-mph wind from 12 o'clock
.44 Rem. Mag. 240-gr. (1,200 fps)	100	13.55/00	13.73/8.54	13.93/00
	200	59.52/00	60.96/31.07	62.51/00
	300	145/00	149.7/65.17	154.8/00
	400	276.9/00	287.8/110.2	299.9/00
	500	462.7/00	483.8/166.4	507.6/00
.220 Swift 55-gr. (3,900 fps)	100	1.24/00	1.24/1.68	1.24/00
	200	5.38/00	5.39/7.05	5.41/00
	300	13.21/00	13.26/16.69	13.32/00
	400	25.77/00	25.93/31.39	26.09/00
	500	44.50	44.88/52.21	45.27/00
.30-06 Springfield 180-gr. (2,520 fps)	100	2.87/00	2.87/1.59	2.88/00
	200	12.09/00	12.11/6.58	12.14/00
	300	28.68/00	28.77/15.40	28.86/00
	400	53.87/00	54.12/28.48	54.37/00
	500	89.19/00	89.73/46.34	90.30/00
12 gauge sabot slug 437.5-gr. (1,350 fps)	100	12.13/00	12.37/15.56	12.62/00
	200	57.51/00	59.55/54.88	61.78/00
	300	148.1/00	155.2/113.6	163/00
	400	297.2/00	314.7/192.3	334.6/00
	500	521.1/00	558/293.2	601.3/00

How much will that affect the lateral wind drift? How about the bullet drop?

I don't have a clue.

Neither does anybody else, not with all the variables.

CONSIDER YOUR BULLET TOO

A bullet's energy would seem to play a role as well, and the more energy it has, the better able it is to counteract the effect of the wind. This was illustrated to me while I was hunting prairie dogs in South Dakota with Dave Brown, the marketing director for Pentax Sport Optics.

The prairie dogs were getting spooky, and our average shooting distance was growing at about the same time the wind started to really pick up. The bullets from our .223 Remingtons were being blown 30 inches or more at 400 yards. The gusting winds made predicting the shots tough, and the points of impact were very erratic. Dave broke out his custom .243 Ackley Improved, and with its heavier 80-grain bullets, the effect of the wind was not only much less pronounced, but a lot more consistent and easier to predict. I was spotting for him, and I was amazed at the difference in the amount of wind deflection and in the consistency of that deflection between the .243's 80-grain bullets and the 50-grain bullets we had been using in the .223 Rem.

The computer didn't predict it, and if I hadn't seen it myself, I would not have believed it. A lot of prairie dogs who also weren't true believers learned the same lesson that day.

AN ART IN ITSELF

Shooting in the wind is far more of an art than a science, and the only real way to learn about reading the wind is to get out and shoot in it. A couple of days in a prairie dog town will teach you more than all the theoretical computer programs or printed ballistic tables in the world. If there is a pronounced lack of prairie dogs where you are, simply find a windy place with some good distance and shoot at rocks, clay pigeons, plastic soda bottles full of water or even paper targets, and do it with a variety of firearms. Have a pal watch your hits through a spotting scope and try to evaluate each shot. After a few thousand rounds or so, you may finally start to get a handle on reading wind.

Wind is a factor in the West, to be sure, but that's not the only place where you'll have to deal with it. This Vermont hunter is high on a mountain where the wind also whips, and he is smartly using shooting sticks to steady his hold.

Chapter 8

SHOOTING AT GAME

In theory, shooting at a stationary big game animal should be almost exactly the same as shooting at a target at the same distance. You simply place the crosshairs where they should be to achieve the desired point of impact for the bullet, then execute the shot.

But it doesn't work that way at all. Shooting at big game has much different psychological and physiologic effects on us than when we shoot at an inanimate target. When hunting, we must deal with a flood of emotions and our body's response to them.

A target shooter's goal is to maintain a low heart rate and normal breathing during the shot. Sometimes a big-game hunter is just trying to keep his heart from exploding and is wondering why he can't seem to breathe at all. While the target shooter is using his brain to execute the shot with a methodical, linear thought sequence, often the big-game hunter's brain activity just seized up and slammed to a dead stop.

How to deal with all of it is explained in further detail in the section of this chapter called "Buck Fever." But the key is to always strive to control your thinking process. The panic that rears its ugly head in these situations is big game's best friend. Before you yank on the trigger, thinking that perhaps the crosshairs might wobble by the kill zone when the gun fires (hey, it could happen!), take a deep breath or two, calm down and *think*.

This is where you have been working so hard to arrive; don't blow it during the end game. A second or two to collect yourself is far better than years and years of regret.

HITTING RUNNING GAME

The best advice anyone can give to most hunters about shooting at running game is simply ... don't!

The ethical questions of shooting at unwounded, but running, game have long been the subject of debate in the hunting world. I can make a strong case for not shooting, but what's the point? The reality is that sooner or later, almost any hunter is going to be faced with a situation where he or she will take a shot at a moving big-game animal. So, while my caution is to avoid shooting at running, unwounded game at all costs, I accept the reality that almost everybody does it at one time or another.

WHY DO WE DO IT

I once did a survey of game wardens in the U.S. and Canada about the ethical and legal aspects of "twice-shot" deer. That is, a deer that one hunter may have shot, but after being hit ran far enough for another hunter to shoot it as well. One game warden wrote back that "the ethics of the situation will change in direct proportion to the size of the buck." So too will the ethics of shooting at running game change in response to outside factors, and a big factor is the trophy quality of the game.

The other side of the issue is that with certain hunting styles, running shots are a fact of life. For example, many still-hunters or trackers (both methods that are popular with Northeastern whitetail hunters) will find that a high percentage of their opportunities are with moving game. And with all our modern-day hand-wringing and apologetic guilt aside, we must admit that the reality is what generations of hunters before us knew and accepted—that an accomplished shooter who knows what he is doing (of which there are precious few in today's hunting world) can take many running shots with good confidence and a clear conscience. In that light,

the most sensible approach would be to learn and practice for the shot you swear you will never take.

GETTING INTO THE DETAILS

I have a fairly extensive collection of shooting literature as well as most of the current computer programs for shooting. The books provide instruction on shooting at running game, and the computers will calculate leads for those shots. For example, the computer will explain that if a whitetail is running at a 90-degree angle to you and is 225 yards distant, if you are shooting a .280 Rem. with 140-grain factory loads, you must lead the point you wish to hit by exactly 13 feet. Pretty cool, don't you think?

Pretty useless too.

What if the buck is actually at an 80-degree angle? Or 85 degrees? Can you tell the difference? While deer can run 35 miles per hour, perhaps this buck is loafing along at a leisurely 26 mph. Or maybe he is the Carl Lewis of whitetails and is hitting 38 mph. What if there is a 15-mph crosswind coming from a 65-degree angle? Are you sure it is 225 yards, not 229? Perhaps you have a .30-06 that day instead of a .280 Rem. Would you know where to hold in any of these situations?

You could easily run the scenarios in the computer and memorize the answers. If you had no life and no place else to spend your time, you might even memorize hundreds or perhaps thousands of formulas, maybe even enough to cover all possible scenarios. But can you judge in an instant the exact angle, speed and distance of any running deer you see? Can you calculate the wind speed and direction and their effects on the bullet?

Maybe you can if you are the Rainman, but if your mind works that fast, you need to spend some time in Las Vegas.

Even if you can memorize the numbers, how can you be sure that you are holding exactly 8 feet 9 inches (or whatever) in front of the lungs? Are you certain it's not 8 feet 3 inches? If your hand-eye coordination and judgment is that sharp, how come you are not playing in the NBA? You can memorize the numbers, but nobody can make them work in the real world. Sure, they provide a guideline, but that's not enough. You need to build on that.

Most aspects of rifle shooting require a methodical, reasoned, thinking approach. Shooting well with a rifle is a fixed mechanical process that requires the shooter to think about what he is doing and that every step be executed in a precise manner. Try that on running game and you'll be disappointed.

ANOTHER "ART"

Shooting well at running game requires a more esoteric approach and the use of a different part of your brain. I remember well one shotgun shooting coach who was becoming visibly agitated with my insistence on using "rifle shooting" techniques for sporting clays. I'll never forget how he snarled at me, "You have the greatest computer on earth sitting on your shoulders, but you won't let it work!"

Once I understood that shotgun shooting required that I allow a different part of my brain to function, I started breaking targets. That coach was watching me shoot some years later when I was having a good day, and afterward he stopped me to offer congratulations.

"You were one of my most frustrating students," he said. "Those rifles just about ruined you. It was a trial for both of us, but I can see it paid off."

You couldn't buy a bigger smile or a better feeling than I had when I walked away from that compliment.

Shooting at running game with a rifle requires a similar technique. You must learn to let your "computer" work its magic. When you put your hand on a hot stove you don't stop and think, "This is hot; I should take my hand off." Instead, you yank your hand away. It's that part of your brain making you take your hand off the stove that you need to use. The difficulty is that for all your rifle-shooting life, you have used the more logical part of your brain. That part might say, "This is hot; I should remove my hand" if you had not already reacted. Making the transition is not easy, but it can be learned.

The ethical questions of shooting at unwounded but running game have long been the subject of debate in the hunting world. The reality is that sooner or later almost any hunter is going to be faced with a situation where he will take a shot at a moving big game animal.

It's like in martial arts; if you must think about your next move, it's already too late to make it. The move must be automatic and controlled by the same subconscious part of your mind that moves your hand off the stove. It doesn't matter if it's martial arts or shooting at moving targets, it doesn't just happen. It takes months and years of practice—practice that builds muscle memory and conditions your mind to what the move should be. Rather than logically thinking about each step, you must develop the ability to let your mind go into a "Zen-like" state so that the unconscious part—again, the part that moves your hand from the stove—is doing the shooting.

You still must, of course, be aware of the sight position, trigger control and all the thousand other things that make for good shooting, but turn off the thinking part of your mind and let that all run on automatic pilot. You should have done enough shooting by now that the trigger control and sight picture are automatic and you don't need to think about them. If you have done that much shooting, then you have built muscle memory through repeating the process over and over, and your body knows what to do.

PRACTICE IS KEY

Doing any shooting well requires lots of burned powder. You must practice until you are able to fire your rifle as an extension of your body. Only then is it wise to practice on moving targets. Once you start, it will take a lot more burned powder before you can hit the targets well. I have seen men good enough to shoot clay pigeons out of the air. But they didn't get there overnight; it took practice, and lots of it.

I used to spend a lot of my winters hunting coyotes with hound dogs. One cold, clear morning, I was sitting on a powerline that was a favorite escape route, waiting for the dogs to strike, when a big coyote just happened to come wandering by and sit down to look at me. At 250 yards, a coyote that is sitting and facing you is not a very big target, and I missed. By the time I racked another shell into my Model 700 .243 Win., the coyote had the afterburners kicked in and was heading for the safety of the woods. The next shot was behind him. I worked the bolt again, and without thinking, I allowed my subconscious mind to take over. The third shot went off without my realizing that I had pulled the trigger, and the 85-grain Sierra took out both his lungs when he was just five feet short of his escape.

I can't tell you how fast he was running, the exact angle or distance or how far I led him, but I could have told you when the trigger sear broke that he was dead. I knew the shot was good before the bullet left the barrel.

It's that wonderful computer perched on my neck being allowed to work its magic.

A DEER HUNTING STORY

When I made my first Western hunt in Montana many years ago, I didn't know a thing about how it all worked.

One bitter cold morning, there was a big mule deer buck running up the far side of a wide canyon, and I thought he looked like a keeper. As was pre-agreed, I kept waiting for the guide to pass judgment until finally the buck was so far away that I figured I had misjudged and he must be too small to even comment on.

"Holy s...," said my young and questionably competent guide. "I just got him in my spotting scope; he's good, shoot him." (He was good, but not that good, raising more questions about the guide's competency.)

As I said, I didn't have a clue. If he said shoot, it must be close enough, so I started shooting. At my first shot, he kicked like a mule.

"You got him; stop shooting," said the guide. But I don't believe in stopping until the game is down. Besides, I saw the bullet strike the snow behind the buck, and I knew it was too far back. I shot twice more, and the 7mm Mag. was empty. I was scrambling for more ammo when the guide, who was still looking though the spotting scope, commented, "Nice shooting; he's down."

"Huh?" I said. "I hit that deer?!"

It turns out that the first shot went through the spot on the buck's rear leg between the tendon and bone that you would cut to put the gamble in to hang a deer. The next two hit his lungs.

Somebody asked me where I was holding for those shots, and before I could tell him, I had to remember back to the mental picture of where the crosshairs were when the gun went off. The other hunters asked how I knew to hold there, but I couldn't answer—except that in thinking back, I realized that after seeing the first shot hit the snow, my mind made the necessary adjustments for the next two shots.

I have hunted a lot in the years since and have learned. Today I would never take that shot; it wouldn't be ethical. But you know something? That buck looks pretty good hanging behind me on my office wall.

Your brain is the best and fastest computer possible for making the adjustments needed to hit running game; let it do its work. This Montana buck is a perfect example—after one shot, the follow-ups both hit their marks.

HITTING RUNNING GAME UP CLOSE—GRAMP'S ADVICE

My grandfather, Nathan Ransom Towsley, was an auto mechanic who owned and operated a garage and gas station to earn his living, but his life was defined by shooting and hunting. Of that, whitetail hunting was his favorite.

He was fond of saying that in his prime, he needed only two days to kill a buck. One to find the deer, the second to shoot a buck. He hunted Vermont in its glory years as abandoned farmland grew back to forest during the 1940s, '50s and '60s. It was ideal whitetail habitat—thick, brushy and full

of deer. Treestands were unheard of and would have brought scorn if one showed up in his deer camp. Back then, real men hunted on their legs, moving along the deers' ground, one-on-one with them. That prevalent hunting style meant a lot of shots at running deer. Gramp was also fond of saying that in those days, if he could see a deer for three jumps, he could put a bullet in him.

As the man said, "It ain't bragging if you can do it!" And Gramp could. Like most good field shots, he had lightning reflexes and excellent eyes. He never even wore glasses until he was in his sixties. He also possessed what today we would call good "eye-hand coordination." Gramp loved to shoot and did a lot of it, so he knew it well; when a deer jumped up, there was no fumbling with the gun; it was all instinctive.

THE CONCEPTS

Gramp taught me early about shooting at running deer up close. "It's thick here, lots of trees and little open air for the bullet to pass through," he told me. "If you want to hit a running buck in this country, pick an opening in the woods just a little bit ahead of him and point your gun at it where you think he will be as he comes through. Watch the sights, but keep looking for the buck with the corner of your eye. When he enters your sight picture, pull the trigger. If you miss, don't try to chase him with your rifle, shooting trees and wasting all your bullets; get on the next opening, hold the rifle still and do it all again."

"Focus on the sights; you still have to aim, but let your brain figure the lead. Don't try to think about it too much; your eyes and head know how to make it work."

"Now, don't think you can just go

If you want to hit a running buck in this country, pick an opening in the woods just a little bit ahead of him and point your gun where you think he will be.

out and do this with the first buck you shoot at; nobody is born a good shot. You need to practice with your rifle. Take your empty rifle out into the woods with you when you are walking around. (Today we call it "scouting.") Follow flushing partridge (grouse), rabbits, deer, squirrels, birds and whatever else you can find. Right now, you are swinging the rifle with them. You are not shooting at them, only trying to learn how to use the scope. Keep practicing until you can follow a flushing partridge or a running rabbit without losing sight of him in your scope.

"Make absolutely sure that gun is empty, then start to practice shooting at them by dry-firing. Pick an opening ahead of them, just like I told you. Dry-fire the gun; it won't hurt your rifle any. After a while, it will begin to come

For running shots, many thick woods hunters like the lightning fast handling of a light carbine like this Winchester Model 94 in .44 Magnum.

together in your head, and your brain will know when to pull the trigger.

"Then get somebody to roll an old tire with plywood in the center down a hill, and try to hit the middle of the plywood. Do it in the woods, if you can, where you have some trees to get in your way; you'll see what I am talking about. It's not the same as a buck charging through the brush, but it's the best we can do, and any practice helps you to get better. Even still, you are going to miss some bucks before you figure it all out, and even a few after you do."

ONE LAST CARTRIDGE

Gramp knew what he was talking about, and in 70 years of deer hunting, he didn't miss many. In addition to the ammo in his belt, he always carried a single extra round in his right-hand coat pocket. He did this because it was easily accessible if he needed it in a hurry. The ammo belt was often under his jacket and hard to get at, but he could always reach the pocket, and he made sure that it contained only that shell and nothing else to get in the way. I don't think that he ever was in a situation where the ammo in the gun couldn't finish the job he started, but it's the little things that count, and the shell was there if he needed it.

At camp the night before the season opened, Gramp would always mark the shell with his knife, making a shallow X on the end of the bullet. He said it was for good luck. So when he died, I marked a bullet the same way and slipped it into the right-hand pocket of his suit jacket just before they buried him.

METHODS OF SHOOTING RUNNING GAME

There are basically three ways to handle your rifle while shooting at running game. They are not unlike shotgun shooting, except instead of a large pattern of shot, you are firing a single bullet and so must be more precise. You are also usually shooting at targets that are farther away. Because of these two factors, to achieve success, you must always use the sights on the rifle.

POINT-SHOOTING

To do this, you shoot with a stationary rifle at a spot ahead of the target where you think the animal will be when the bullet arrives. Generally, this is done by throwing the rifle to your shoulder as you focus your vision on the spot and then shooting as soon as the rifle hits the right place and the sights look right. You are predicting where the target will be at a point in the future that will coincide with the bullet's arrival and aiming at that spot. For this to work correctly, you must fire the instant the sights look right. Any hesitation at all will cause you to shoot behind the animal.

This works well for shooting at close-range moving targets, particularly in thick brush. It helps a great deal to have a rifle that fits you correctly and hits your shoulder with the sights lined up perfectly with your eye. Without a perfect fit, your eye needs to search for the sights. Even if it takes only a moment, it will take enough time to likely cause a miss.

SWING-THROUGH

With this method, the hunter starts with the rifle behind the running target. By swinging the rifle faster than the game is moving, the sights will pass by the target, and when the forward lead is correct, the shooter fires the rifle. The timing requires anticipating when the lead will be correct and shoot-

Safely Shooting Running Game

There is an inherent danger in shooting at running game in that the shooter tends to focus on the animal and block out the rest of the surroundings. When the target is moving and the rifle is moving with it, this can be very dangerous.

It is far too easy to shoot your hunting partner as you swing the gun, failing to notice that he or she is standing in the path. This is a common scenario for hunting accidents. The hunter is following a fleeing deer, and just as the hunter pulls the trigger, the partner's head appears in the scope. Both are focusing on the same deer and never even notice until it's too late.

It's also easy to block out the background behind the fleeing target and to swing the gun in an unsafe direction. With today's increasing urbanization of hunting areas, this is even more critical. Even if no damage is done and no one gets hurt, the sport of hunting has another black eye.

Always remain fully aware of what you are doing, where everybody else is and what lies in the direction you are moving the rifle muzzle. Never let your focus on the shot become so complete that you fail to realize where the muzzle of your rifle is pointing at all times. So what if it means that the animal gets away from you? There is no deer or elk worth the risk of shooting somebody.

The power of destruction from a modern rifle bullet is catastrophic, particularly at close range. Once that bullet leaves the barrel, you can never take it back. Make sure it doesn't become a nightmare. Never let the moment allow you to forget safety. Pay attention at all times.

Red-Dot & Holo Sights

You might consider one of the many red-dot electronic sights or the Bushnell Holo Sight as an alternative to a scope or iron sights.

Both are extremely fast to use and can be a big asset for shooting at running game. The red-dot features an electronically generated aiming point that "floats" in the viewing area of the sight. Adequate eye relief is unlimited, and there is no parallax. If you can see the dot and put it on the target, you will hit it. If you doubt that red-dots are very fast, go visit a handgun shooting competition where speed is the primary scoring system and see what the top competitors are using.

There will be red-dot sights on virtually every gun in the winner's circle.

The Bushnell Holo Sight is similar in that it uses a holographic aiming point that is floated in front of the shooter's eye. It borrows from the "heads up" aiming technology of jet fighters. It's fast enough that I have successfully shot trap with one mounted on a shotgun.

With these systems, you can keep both eyes open and "see" the aiming point floating over the target. If your style of hunting calls for close shooting of any kind, but particularly quick shooting up close, check these sights out.

To achieve a sustained lead properly: Maintain a constant lead—at the same perceived speed as the game—and keep the rifle moving as you pull the trigger and follow through.

ing a little before that to allow for shooter lag time as well as the lock time for the rifle.

The rifle is kept moving the entire time, until well after the shot and follows through. If you stop moving the rifle when the sight picture looks right, you will shoot behind the target. You must keep the gun moving and fire without hesitation when the sights are at the correct amount of lead. Hesitation with a moving gun will cause you to shoot in front of the target, because the gun will swing past the correct lead before firing.

SUSTAINED LEAD

The gun is moved with the target at the same perceived speed. The proper lead is attained and retained, and the rifle is kept moving through the shot and follow-through.

This is my preferred method for long-range shooting at moving targets. I think it is easier to maintain a constant lead than to shoot during the very short instant when the lead is correct, which is necessary when using the swing-through or point-shooting style of shooting.

RUNNING GAME PRACTICE

The most commonly suggested way to practice shooting at moving targets is to put a piece of plywood in the center of an old tire and have somebody roll it down a hill for you. It helps if the terrain is a little rough so that the tire bounces unpredictably as it rolls. When the plywood gets shot up, you can staple paper over it so you can see your bullet holes (or lack of them!).

Make sure you have a safe place to do this with a good backstop and that the tire is well away from your buddy who is rolling it before you start shooting. My friends and I use a flag that the tire must pass before we can shoot. Actually, the best way is to have several tires so that you can shoot at more than one before collecting them to bring back to the top of the hill. A four-wheeler is pretty handy for that chore.

In a moderate wind, releasing balloons and shooting at them as they skid along the ground is good practice; just make sure you clean up afterward.

Finally, as you become better, try shooting at clay pigeons either thrown from a hand trap or with a small automatic

The most commonly suggested way to practice shooting at moving targets is to put a piece of plywood in the center of an old tire and have somebody roll it down a hill for you.

trap. Start with the target going away from you; then, as you get better, have somebody throw them from various angles. (Again, only where there is a solid, safe backdrop. Rifle bullets can be dangerous for a long distance.)

It's not easy, and you won't break them all—or even a majority of them. But if you reach a level of proficiency where you are breaking almost as many as you are missing of these little targets, a buck's chest is going to look pretty big in your sights.

It helps if the terrain is a little rough so that the tire bounces unpredictably as it rolls.

BUCK FEVER

I remember years ago, back when my little brother Scott was still in junior high school, he came home from deer hunting one afternoon, near tears and looking for me. It turns out he shot at a buck up in the woods we knew locally as "Sherwin's." I guess "shot at" is an understatement—he emptied the old Marlin lever-action .38-55. A buddy who was hunting close by said it sounded like a Gatling gun fighting off an Indian attack.

"He was huge!" Scott exclaimed. "I couldn't have missed him! He was right on top of me, just standing there looking around and acting all confused."

Morning found us standing by a pile of empty brass. We looked for hours, following track after track in the dusting of snow, but there was no evidence he put a bullet anywhere near the deer.

"Where were you aiming?" I asked.

"I don't know."

"You don't remember?"

"I remember fine, I just don't know."

"Did you even look at the sights?"

"I don't think so."

"What were you doing while you were shooting?"

"Mostly shaking."

It was as classic a case of buck fever as I have witnessed in 30-plus years of deer hunting, and trust me, I have seen a few.

GETTING UPTIGHT

It can happen to the best of us. You work day after day to shoot a deer. It's something you want more than anything else in life, and it seems like it's never going to happen. Nothing you can do will force it to happen. You can't buy a deer, and sometimes hard work isn't enough to earn one. It's frustrating because you simply don't know what else you can do. You keep working at it day after day while the hollow pain in the pit of your stomach keeps snickering to your brain that you will never shoot another deer. Then without warning, he's there in front of you, and it's time.

Suddenly, your arms won't stop shaking, your knees won't support your weight and it's getting really hard to breathe. You've planned for the moment, worked it all out in your mind a thousand times, but now your brain isn't responding. You can't think, you can't breathe, your peripheral vision has deserted you and nothing is working right. Everything on your gun has moved and is in the wrong place, and it looks like he is going to get away.

Think it can't ever happen to you? Don't bet on it.

BEATING THE AFFLICTION

So how do you beat "buck fever"?

That's a question that hunters have been wrestling with since they were chucking stone-headed spears. The very best thing I know is to do a lot of hunting. Experience seems to help more than anything else. Beyond that, there are a few things you can do to prepare.

Be ready, know your equipment and have confidence in your ability. An awful lot of bucks are still alive because the hunter started second-guessing himself about the shot. Even

Nine-year-old Nathan Towsley, the author's son, admits he got a little buck fever on his first whitetail buck. This was one of three trees he hit, but as he points out, "The important thing is that I got the deer!"

more deer owe their lives to hunters who couldn't find the safety. Know your gun, and believe in your ability and that knowledge. You get there by shooting a lot before the season, practicing for the one shot that will count.

When I first see a deer I want to shoot, I usually start to shake and my respiration rate shoots though the roof. But I have taught myself to mentally calm down enough to make the shot. When it's time to shoot, regardless if it is 10 seconds after I first see the deer or 10 minutes, I can usually get my mind and body into a "zone" where I calm down, bring my heart rate and breathing to a manageable level and can mentally concentrate on shooting. I forget how much I want the deer or how big his antlers are; I just concentrate on the shot.

Of course after it's all over, I fall apart!

Expect to see a deer (or whatever you're hunting), visualize shooting it in your mind's eye … and you'll have a better chance of conquering buck fever when the real thing makes an appearance. Then you'll get to drag it out.

STEPS TO TAKE

This is not an easy thing, and several factors have contributed to my control. First is lots of hunting. I now have 33 big-game seasons behind me, and I have hunted in 26 states and 10 Canadian provinces. I spend about 150 days a year hunting something. I still get buck fever and I still blow it once in a while, but not as often as I once did.

Another thing that helped a great deal was bowhunting. When you hunt with a rifle, a deer can usually be taken very soon after it's spotted. But bowhunting is a close-range deal. Often, you will watch a buck a long time before a shot presents itself. By the time that happened, I was usually a quivering mass of drooling idiot and missed so many deer that I could fill a book with those stories alone. It came down to learning to control it, or accepting that I would never succeed and quit bowhunting. I chose to learn some control.

Being around a lot of deer helps, but not much. There is a big difference between a deer you want to shoot and those you are simply looking at. Hanging around deer you truly want to shoot is the key.

One more thing that I think helped a lot was competitive shooting. There were times when I wanted to win a match as badly as I ever wanted any buck. Inevitably, those were the times when I lost.

I learned to control my emotions and to focus on shooting. To concentrate only on the shot at hand, not to worry about anything else. Then I started winning. You can't do this with casual practice; it has to count for a lot and be something you want so badly it hurts. Another aspect of this was the crowd that watched me shoot. The pressure of doing it in front of a lot of people manifested itself in symptoms that mimicked buck fever almost exactly.

Finally, visualizing the shot in your mind over and over before you ever see the deer will help. Athletes use this technique to prepare; so can hunters. In your mind, see yourself shooting a buck. Make him a big one, so if the real buck that shows up is huge, you are ready for that too. Walk through it in your mind's eye, step by step, and do it again and again. While you are sitting in your stand, pick a place where you think a buck will appear. Then put him there in your mind and visualize the process of fighting off buck fever and shooting the deer. Move to the next spot you might see a deer and do it again. Do this over and over, and when the real thing finally appears, your mind will be conditioned to pull it off. Or at least have a better chance of pulling it off; there are never any guarantees with buck fever.

A PART OF LIVING THE HUNT

One more thing about buck fever. It signifies the importance we place on hunting and indicates what it means not only to our hearts, but also to our souls. If we didn't care, if it were easy, it wouldn't be worth much. Buck fever is a reminder of that.

I hope it never stops. The day I fail to start breathing fast at the sight of a big buck, I'll quit hunting.

TAKE A REST

A heavy frost lent the appearance of a light snow-fall to the south Alabama clearcut, and while not exactly common in this locality, it comforted this misplaced Northern deer hunter. The three does that fled in panic from the first notes of my rattling horns had done little to boost my confidence, but the place looked so perfect that I continued strumming them a little longer than usual.

After nearly an hour, though, I gave it up, tied the horns together and stood up to leave. A flicker of movement caught my eye, and a quick check with binoculars revealed an eye framed by four points on a single antler. With the rest of the buck hidden behind a tree, I couldn't shoot if I want-ed to, and right then I didn't really want to.

I had expected the shot to be closer, and with 250 yards of Southern air between us, I didn't dare take an offhand shot. That eye was watching me watch him, and when the deer turned to sneak down his backtrail, I waited until his head went behind the tree before I made my move. I stepped for-ward and snugged the rifle against another tree that had been just out of reach. I picked the only open hole in the brush ahead of him, which at the time looked about the size of a golf ball. When his shoulder entered the "hole," I squeezed the trigger.

It took a while and a little of my cousin Stephen Baker's confidence in my shooting before we found him. I had misjudged where he was and had been looking on the wrong side of a big pool of standing water. I was ready to quit, but Stephen insisted that if I felt the shot was good, I had probably hit him. I finally waded the water, and just far enough beyond so we couldn't see it was a blood trail that left no doubt.

That was a long time ago, and as I recall, it was the first game I ever shot with a .300 Win. Mag. It was not, however, the first time I had waited to shoot until I could find a rest, nor would it be the last. The buck was leaving and so conveyed a sense of urgency to start shooting, but I am convinced that if I had succumbed to the temptation to plug away at him offhand, I would have missed.

TAKE THE TIME TO FIND A REST

Except for game jumped at close range, it's rare in a hunting situation that you can't find a rest for your rifle before shooting. Any shooter, no matter what the skill level, will do better if a rest is used. Leave the demonstrations of marksmanship from human-supported positions at the target range. When you are hunting, you owe it to the animal you are shooting, to the sport and to yourself to minimize the variables.

Whenever it's possible, and it almost always is, find a rest. Usually, that simply means locating a handy tree or rock to brace the rifle against. Lacking that, you can use your backpack if there is time. I did just that in northern British Columbia on my first moose. It was a long shot, but I never

doubted for a moment that I could hit him. When the trigger broke, that .375 H&H Mag. was as steady as the proverbial rock.

SHOOTING STICKS

If I am hunting in the woods, I rarely worry about finding a rest; there is always something within a few steps. But in

Where trees, rocks and other potential rests are few and far between, shooting sticks make an excellent rest.

Take the time to find a rest. Any rest. This antelope hunter is using a fencepost. It's not fancy, but it's solid and it sure gets the job done.

places where trees and the like are hard to come by, I bring my own. There are several portable rests on the market, but the style I like best is the modern-day version of the old crossed-stick standby. Traditionally, these are simply two finger-sized-diameter sticks that are sharpened on one end. They are crossed near the other end and tied to form a hinge. The bottoms are spread apart and planted in the ground, while the cross forms a V at the top into which the rifle is nestled. With practice, a shooter can grasp the sticks and the rifle while applying tension toward his body and become remarkably steady.

The "modern" version is simply a set of aluminum "sticks" that are shock-corded together like a tent pole. By separating the sections, you can fold them up for carry. All that's necessary to get them into action is to grab the top and shake. The sections will fall into place and the cords will pull them together.

I like the length designed for shooting while sitting down because I feel it's a lot steadier and handier than standing. However, there are some circumstances where the standing-height sticks are needed. In places where vegetation is too high to shoot from sitting and there are no other rests, these taller crossed sticks would be most valuable.

BIPOD

Another popular type of rest is a bipod that attaches to your rifle, usually on the front swivel stud. I love these for varmint shooting, but I really don't like them much for most big-game hunting, largely because they change the balance of the gun too

much. Carrying a rifle slung on your shoulder with one installed can be frustrating. The weight added to the front of the rifle will cause the gun to keep rolling back and falling off your shoulder.

I did say *most* big-game hunting, though. Attachable bipods are perhaps the steadiest type of portable rest, and for deer or pronghorns on the open prairie, where long shots are all but a guarantee, that bonus more than offsets the inconvenience of carrying a rifle with a bipod attached. Again, I like the model that allows shooting from a sitting position.

A popular type of rest is a bipod that attaches to your rifle, usually on the front swivel stud.

FIELD POSITIONS

There are four basic shooter-supported field positions that hunters will fire from: standing, sitting, kneeling and prone. As practical shooting positions for hunting, they all have their place, but of course, each also has its unique strong points and weaknesses.

The key with them all is to always try to have bone rather than muscle supporting the rifle. The old adage is to "build a bridge of bones." Bone is solid and immovable, while muscle is soft, flexible and subject to tremors. Obviously, if you are among the living, your bones are covered with soft tissue. Think of this as padding for the structural support, like the foam on a rifle rest. Visualize a solid, internal structural bridge of supporting bone between the rifle and the ground. Any time you interrupt that structure with supporting muscle, you induce more movement and less control.

STANDING OR OFFHAND

Standing up and shooting "on your hind legs" is absolutely the worst position for most hunting. But I'll wager that well over half the big-game critters shot at are dodging bullets fired by a standing hunter. I'll also wager that more big-

You'll always shoot better with some kind of rest—any kind of rest—versus shooting offhand.

Kneeling is one way you can be ready to shoot in an instant, in fast-action situations such as rattling.

game critters owe their continued existence to so many hunters' insistence of shooting from this position than to any other single aspect of shooting.

That said, often it's the only option. When the shot must be taken fast, or when vegetation or terrain prevents using other positions, the hunter must shoot offhand. If you took this option away, the deer kill in New England would plummet. Many a still-hunter or tracker has never killed a deer from any other position.

Further, this position is extremely helpful because it will teach a shooter a lot about the art of field shooting, and for that reason alone, it should be practiced often. It's rare for a truly good field shot not to also be a good offhand shot as well. To become one, a shooter must learn the discipline of trigger control, how to control sight wobble and the relationship between the two. If a shooter can shoot well from standing, he can do it very well from any other position.

One reason standing is such a poor position to shoot from is that it is almost impossible to build that bridge of bones. Competitive shooters come close by using fore-end extensions with palm rests or weird-looking positions that allow the elbow of the left hand (for right-hand shooters) to be wedged against the hip. None of that really works well for a hunter. In the end, you will find that the muscles of your left shoulder and arm are supporting the rifle. You can build a little tension by pulling back with that hand as you push forward with your right shoulder, and that helps steady the gun and calm your muscles. But you can't escape that it's still

muscle supporting the rifle. Not only that, but you are holding the rifle the farthest from the ground possible to still aim. As a rule of thumb, the closer to the ground you can put the rifle, the steadier the position will become.

Stand at an angle to the target, usually close to 90 degrees, with your left shoulder facing the target. Your feet should be shoulder-width apart with the left foot pointed slightly to the target. The key is to find a position that is solid and comfortable. Snug the gun butt into the pocket formed between the muscle of your shoulder and your collarbone. Do not put the rifle butt on your collarbone or on your bicep. This pocket helps steady the rifle but also puts a little meat behind it to absorb the recoil. This will vary a bit with body type, so you may have to experiment some to find what works best for you.

The right elbow should be about parallel with the ground. Keep the left arm under the rifle, much like a waiter carrying a large tray. This again keeps bone supporting the rifle as much as possible. If the arm is held out to the side, as many shooters try to do, you are depending more on muscle to hold the weight of the rifle.

KNEELING

This may be a competitive shooting position, but in my opinion, it's a poor way to shoot a rifle at game. In theory, it should be more stable than standing, but I have never been able to shoot well while kneeling.

Because kneeling also puts your line of sight nearly as low as sitting, and considering that sitting is a far superior shooting position, I see little use for kneeling in the field. Some say it's faster than sitting, and I suppose that may have some merit. But if you use kneeling rather than sitting because it saves you half a second, what do you have? Usually just a faster miss.

Once again, use the concept of bones supporting the rifle. Your left knee will be up, pointing at the target and supporting your left arm. Don't put the elbow directly on the knee; that's wobbly, and it's always slipping off. Instead, find a comfortable position where the edge of the elbow and upper forearm are against the knee.

I can't bend my right foot nearly enough to sit on the side of it as competitive shooters do in the "low kneeling position," and because I have rather bulky muscles in my legs, I simply bend my right leg until it won't bend any more and use that to support my weight as I sit on it. Other body types will again have to find what's comfortable for them.

Slump your body forward and arch your back to lower your center of gravity. It helps to build a little muscle tension between the left knee and left arm. Keep your arm under the rifle so that the bones of your arm and leg are supporting the weight.

In theory it should be more stable than standing, but many hunters find kneeling a poor way to shoot a rifle.

PRONE

This is said to be the most stable shooter-supported position for a rifleman. I have watched the best Olympic shooters up close, and a good prone shooter can shoot almost as well as from a benchrest.

But not me.

I don't like prone for several reasons. First is that it rarely works in the field. It simply puts you too low to the ground, and there is always something in the way when you try to shoot. Even if you think the path is clear, remember that the bullet's path is initially lower than your line of sight. I recall one caribou hunter shooting several times at a nice bull from a prone position. I was watching the caribou through my binoculars but couldn't see where the bullets were striking. Finally, the bull tired of the game and wandered off. We decided to walk out there just to make sure he hadn't hit the foolish thing, and about 20 feet in front of the shooter was a boulder with its top well scarred and marked from repeated .30-06 bullets skidding across it.

I mostly don't like shooting prone because I am not built right for it. I have a very short and large neck. (Some say I have no neck at all and that my head sits directly on my shoulders.) I also have a rather thick torso. With the two combined, I find it very awkward to shoot from a prone position, a complaint echoed by other hunters. (In spite of the rumors, it is not true that I am just as apt to start rocking on my belly and fall asleep.)

I can easily count on one hand the big-game animals I have shot from the prone position—and have fingers left over. Or I could simply count the layers of scar tissue over my right eye, because I think every one of those shots left me bleeding from the scope hitting me in the face. The prone position puts your face forward on the rifle stock and close to the scope. That not only creates problems with the eye relief of most scopes and results in less than a full field of

A good prone shooter can shoot almost as well as from a bench rest. In places like the wide-open plains, shooting prone is often the only option.

The sitting position is the rifle hunter's best friend. It gets him up above the vegetation, steadies the rifle, and allows him to absorb the recoil without lasting physical damage.

view, but it also shortens the distance the scope needs to travel to draw blood.

I remember very well my best elk, which I shot with a .338 Win. Mag. from the prone position. When it was over, I left a better blood trail than he did.

But for those who can work it, prone is steady and for that reason alone is a useful position. The traditional hunting position is for the shooter to lie on the ground with his or her body at a 45-degree angle to the target. This allows the body to act like a spring and flex a little more under recoil, absorbing and dispersing the force. Many shooting coaches teach the shooter to lie more in line with the rifle, but they are usually shooting .22 rifles. The more directly behind the rifle you are, the more your body will feel the full effect of the recoil. If you are into taking the full kick of something like a .340 Wthby Mag., you probably have a great future in full-contact karate.

Keep your elbows close together and in front of you. The left one should be under the rifle, supporting it. Again, support the rifle with bone. Position your legs so they are comfortable. It sometimes helps to cock the left leg up a little and put tension on the muscles of the leg and back.

SITTING

This position is the rifle hunter's best friend. It gets you above the vegetation, steadies the rifle and allows you to

absorb the recoil without lasting physical damage. It is, for all practical purposes, quick to assume and easy to move around if the animal changes positions before you can shoot.

Sit at about a 45-degree angle to the target. You can cross your legs at the ankles in front of you or simply plant your feet side by side on the ground. Actually, you may find yourself using both styles as the situation dictates. Don't place the points of your elbows on the points of your knees. This is both painful and wobbly. Instead, use the flats of your arms against the flats of your legs in any way that fits your body style well.

Different body types will use slightly different positions, and all hunters have to work it out for themselves. But again, think bone support. Personally, I like to cross my legs and hunch my back so I am low to the ground and balled up with the backs of my elbows against the fronts of my knees.

If you can get your back up against something like a tree or log, it steadies you even more. I recently made a rifle shot on a turkey in the Texas Panhandle where the wind could blow the hair off a Longhorn steer. There was no cover, so I braced against my buddy Tad Brown, who is a very big man. Tad helped to anchor me against the wind and my own wobble, and I put the 6mm bullet through the exact feather I wanted to hit at the base of that turkey's neck.

Chapter 9

WHERE TO HIT THEM

An ethical and successful hunter should know the animal he is hunting, literally inside and out. A knowledge of the game's anatomy is important to successful hunting. It is critical that we further understand the biology of the animals we hunt and know the systems that keep them alive. We should know the function and the placement of all the major organs; we must understand why they are potential targets and how to find them in a living animal. A good hunter understands how to locate the target from any viewing angle that allows an ethical shot.

All big game are not created equal, and they are not all built the same. A deer is constructed differently from a bear, just as an elk is put together with a slightly different blueprint than was used for a wild hog. Knowing the location of the major stuff in each of these can make the difference between a clean, one-shot kill and a long, grueling tracking job. Also, by knowing anatomy, we can make judgments on those infrequent hits that went awry and now require that we assess what happened and how to proceed.

Shot placement is critical to success in big-game hunting; of that, there's no room for argument. But it's a simple science with few true target areas. Those who design to play fancy for the sake of bragging rights are not worthy of the title of hunter.

SHOT PLACEMENT ON VARIOUS GAME ANIMALS

Where to hit a big game animal with a rifle bullet has fueled thousands of late-night conversations and led to arguments in hunting camps all over the world.

Variables abound in hunting, and sometimes you must take the shot as it is presented. If all you can see is the neck, then a neck shot it is. But when you have a choice, for the vast majority of hunting situations you need remember only one thing: animals can't live if they can't breathe. The lung shot is by far the most useful and best option in almost every big-game hunting situation.

THE LUNGS HAVE IT

No animal will survive a solid double-lung hit with a quality expanding rifle bullet of the appropriate weight, diameter and velocity for hunting that species. The game may run a little distance, but it won't be far, and if you are using the right equipment, there will be a good blood trail to follow. That trail will always end at a dead animal.

A lung shot generally ruins very little meat, and the lungs provide the largest target with the biggest margin of error of any of the deadly target zones. If you shoot a little low, you should hit the heart. A high bullet will spine the animal. If you are too far behind, you will hit the liver, and you have to move pretty far forward to run out of lungs.

Shooting big game is no time to gamble, and playing to the best odds will have you shooting for the lungs every time. Hunting is neither the time nor place to "prove" your marksmanship. Forget your ego—aim for the biggest and deadliest target and don't take chances.

BROADSIDE SHOTS

With broadside shots, simply follow the back line of the front leg up to the center of the animal and place the bullet there.

Broadside: Follow the back line of the front leg up to the center of the animal's chest. The lungs make a big and lethal target, with a little "breathing room" for high, low or left-right variation in bullet placement.

QUARTERING AWAY

With any quartering-away shot, visualize the off-side shoulder and aim so the bullet will pass through the center of it on its way out of the animal, and the bullet's path will pass through the lungs.

If the animal is quartering severely away from you, this is a shot that should be reserved only for when you have plenty of gun and bullet. It is surprising how much a bullet must penetrate in this circumstance. It will often need to pass through the paunch, which can be full of soggy, partially digested food. Then it will penetrate the liver, hopefully having enough energy left to severely damage the lungs before smashing through the off shoulder and exiting. That's a lot to ask from a bullet.

I have twice tried this shot with marginal calibers and disappointing results. One was a whitetail doe I shot with a 7X30 Waters handgun and 120-grain factory loads. The first bullet stopped in the deer's very full paunch. So did the second. I finally worked around for a broadside shot, and the third bullet penetrated the lungs, ending things. I should note it wasn't a particularly large doe.

The other deer was big and a very nice whitetail buck. I shot him just in front of the hindquarter with a short-barreled 7mm-08 Rem. and 140-grain factory load. It was only about a 50-yard shot, and I had a solid rest. That rifle is very accurate, and I could have predicted which

Quartering away: With an adequate cartridge and bullet, this shot is fine. Aim for the off-side shoulder. That means the bullet will enter just behind his ribs. Imagine you're trying to break his far shoulder.

hairs the bullet would part on the way in. That aiming point would have the bullet break the off shoulder, and since I saw him stumble on that leg, I think it at least hit the shoulder. The trouble is, the bullet never exited. He had only to run a little distance before he was in the standing water of a large and thick swamp. The bullet must have lost a lot of energy before it made it to the lungs, and although it penetrated them, it probably didn't do as much damage as it would have with a broadside shot. With the loss of velocity and energy comes also a loss in hydrostatic shock, which, in fragile lung tissue, can have a substantial effect when shooting high-velocity bullets. The bullet penetrated the lungs, causing a bleedout, and I am certain he died quickly. However, a deer,

even a mortally wounded deer, can cover a lot of ground in a very short time. With no exit wound, there was no followable blood trail, and even though four of us looked for the better part of two days, we never found him.

In both cases, I was using cartridges and bullets that were adequate for deer but obviously not powerful enough to fully penetrate from any direction. The choices come down to passing on this type of shot when using guns that are merely "adequate" for the game, or using something that will penetrate with sufficient remaining energy to kill quickly in a "worst-case scenario." Because I believe hunting opportunities are too hard to come by and because this is one thing I can control, I usually elect to tote a bigger gun. But in the cases where I do not, I exercise control and pass on these hard-quartering shots.

QUARTERING TOWARD

Shots with a quartering animal facing toward you require that you visualize the lungs and try to put the bullet through the center of the animal's chest. The aiming point will vary with the angle from the on-side shoulder to the base of the neck. The temptation for many hunters is to aim behind the shoulder, just as they would for a broadside shot. This will result in the bullet hitting too far back. A paunch-shot deer is always a dead deer because this shot is not survivable with a modern rifle, but often the deer is not recovered. It can suffer a long and painful death, and any humane hunter will strive to avoid this.

STRAIGHT ON & AWAY

Straight-on or straight-away shots are poor to start with, but with enough penetration, the bullet will hit the lungs, although possibly only one. On anything larger than deer, a

Quartering toward: This shot requires that you visualize the lungs and put the bullet through the center. The aiming point is going to be the inside edge of his right shoulder and one third or a bit more up his chest. Imagine you're trying to break the shoulder facing you.

straight-away shot is risky and best to pass on. There is simply too much animal to penetrate for most bullets to pull it off.

When the animal is facing straight at you, the actual kill zone is small, particularly on a deer or pronghorn. The bullet doesn't have to stray much to either side before it simply breaks a leg or gouges a shoulder. It's always best to wait for a better shot; usually your patience will be rewarded.

OTHER SHOTS: ALL TO AVOID

Heart shots are much trickier. It's a far smaller target and harder to visualize inside the animal. Heart shots are, of course, deadly, but it's easy to screw up, hit too low and lose the animal, often with a broken leg that is nothing more than a painful, long-term death sentence.

Intentional spine shots are too risky. It's a very small target top to bottom. Can you hit a 2-inch target every time under field conditions? I know I can't. And that's assuming you even know exactly where to aim. Most hunters will misidentify the location of the spine.

The neck shot is a favorite with many of those campfire experts and can be spectacular in its results. But it can fail miserably too. There is a lot of neck that really isn't all that important to staying alive. If the bullet doesn't hit the spine or the major blood vessels, it can fail to kill the animal.

I know of more than one case when a neck-shot animal got up and ran off. One of my buddies shot a whitetail in the neck with a .30-06, and it fell just like it was supposed to. He leaned his gun up against a tree and pulled out his knife just about the time the buck got up and ran off. Another hunter shot the deer a couple of days later, and when my buddy went to look at the buck, the bullet hole in the neck was right where he had been aiming. The trouble was that it hit only meat.

Straight on: It would be better to wait for a broadside shot, but if you decide to take this shot, place the bullet at the base of his neck, dead center.

Straight away: There is no shot here—whether it's an elk, deer, pronghorn ... any game. To hit the vitals, the bullet would have to travel through the massive hipbone on the right side and it would likely be deflected from its path before reaching the chest cavity. Wait for a better angle.

To Kill a Moose

Moose have huge hearts, big lungs and a lot of blood in their systems, so it takes a while for things to shut down. Even bulls that are well hit will often stay on their feet, mulling it over for a while. You rarely see the spectacular "drop-them-in-their-tracks" kills that you see with deer. If for no other reason, a moose has a lot more body mass to soak up the bullet energy, so those instant "shutdowns" are rare. Even well-hit moose usually move on, if only a little. They have a nasty habit of finally giving it up in the worst possible place, like a muddy bog or in 3 feet of frigid water.

This is one reason for the common reaction from a first-time moose hunter when he approaches his bull and sees 1,000+ pounds of dead moose lying in the mud: "Oh my God, what do I do now?"

With that in mind, it's good strategy to shoot bull moose in the shoulders. Bust some bones, break them down and take away the support structure so the animal can't wander into some soupy nightmare.

Normally a lung shot would be best, but you can't know where this bull will run and it might be a worse place. Try to break him down by aiming to the off-side shoulder, trying to break both of them. Only try this if you have a big cartridge and are shooting heavy, quality bullets.

Just make sure you have enough gun and bullet to pull it off. Those bones are big and tough, and they hide under a lot of muscle.

My grandfather had the same thing happen with a deer he shot in the neck with a .45-70 Gov. The difference was that he noticed what was happening and shot again as the buck regained his feet. This time, he hit him in the lungs.

I detest head shots and think it's a slob hunter's egotistical aiming point. The hunters I know who use them love to brag about it. I think it shows disrespect to the animal and risks too much pain and suffering ever to use. Most hunters need see only one starving, slobbering animal with its bottom jaw smashed from a muffed head shot before they agree with me.

BREAK THE SHOULDER

On game that can bite you, or game that you must anchor on the spot, such as a moose near a bog or a goat on a ledge, a shoulder shot can be effective. This not only takes out the lungs and possibly the heart, but if done right, it breaks the shoulder bones on one or both sides of the animal. By breaking down the support structure, you take away the animal's means of running off. In the case of a grizzly, that can keep him put long enough to die. More than one

fatally shot bear has charged the hunter and had enough juice left to do some serious damage before expiring.

This isn't always 100 percent successful in putting the animal down on the spot, particularly if only one shoulder is broken. However, it is your best chance other than hitting the spine or brain, both small and risky targets.

Just make certain that you have enough bullet and cartridge to pull it off. The bones of truly big game can soak up a lot of bullet energy. A bullet that stops on the shoulder, breaking the bone but failing to continue on to destroy the lungs or the heart, will result only in a wounded animal.

Many arguments for taking risky shots are predicated on "spoiling too much meat." I don't buy it. First off, lung shots spoil very little meat. Secondly, how much meat will spoil if the animal runs off to die later, or if you miss completely?

Shoot them in the lungs and let's argue about something else.

Black Bears: Why They Are Different

Bears, even little bears, can have a dramatic effect on most hunters' shooting ability, always negative.

That leads to problems because the kill zone on a bear is relatively small. Long hair makes a bear appear bigger than he is, and when it's hanging down, it masks the true location of the bottom of his chest. Hunters will often shoot low. Also, from a treestand, the angle of the shot requires that the bullet entry be a little high. A bear's heart is low and further forward than a deer's, and the lungs are smaller. The target zone is actually smaller than on deer and a little more forward in the animal. It's best to try to shoot when the bear is slightly quartering away from you so that you can hit both lungs and to aim for the center of the bear (top to bottom), just slightly behind the shoulder.

On broadside shots, it's better to aim right at the point of the shoulder. Not only will you hit the lungs and possibly the heart, but you will break one or both shoulders, helping to put the bear down more quickly. This is, of course, another reason to use a big cartridge with a heavy bullet. Because bones are tough on bullets, light or inferior-quality bullets can fail to penetrate after smashing through the shoulder.

On hunts over bait, learn how to slide the safety off quietly. A bear can hear extremely well, and hunters are usually close when they first see them. Another thing is to be very quiet moving in and out of the stand; have your gun already loaded (be very careful about safety) because a bear can hear you working the action from a long distance.

A good scope gives you 20 to 25 more minutes of hunting in the evening than you would have with iron sights and it helps a lot with bullet placement, but keep it turned down as low as possible. Too many hunters turn them up to eight or nine power, and when the bear shows up, all they can see is black. They can't tell where they are aiming, and bears are wounded.

For some reason that still escapes me, a lot of wounded bears are hit in the front leg, particularly when they are shot at from treestands. If you find pieces of bone at the site, with a good blood trail leaving that soon peters out, it's probable that the bullet hit the leg, and you are not likely to find that bear.

If you shoot and the bear drops, be careful. Time and again, I have listened to disappointed hunters tell how that happened, and as soon as they worked the action on their rifle or started out of the stand, the bear took off. Bears are so fast that often even if the hunter

The front leg is back, so you will have to drive a bullet through his shoulder or wait until he steps ahead. With a good cartridge and bullet, the shoulder shot is fine. Aim for the point of his near shoulder.

thought he was ready, the bear left before he could fire a second shot. Personally, if a bear drops at the shot, I shoot him again just to be sure. My taxidermist may complain about the extra bullet holes, but I can live with that. At the very least, if the bear drops, keep your rifle on him for a while.

Shot placement is still more important than any other single factor. The best bear gun in the world is worthless if you don't hit the bear in the right place.

Chapter 10

OUR FUTURE HUNTERS

"The little world of childhood with its familiar surroundings is a model of the greater world. The more intensively the family has stamped its character upon the child, the more it will tend to feel and see its earlier miniature world again in the bigger world of adult life."

—*Carl Gustav Jung*

"Train up a child in the way he should go; and when he is old, he will not depart from it."

—*Proverbs 22:6*

How we measure a person's life and its impact on the world is a question that will be debated for as long as humans endure. We can't all be huge historical figures, and the measurement for the common person is often more subtle, but no less important. Perhaps one critical clue can be found in the legacy a person leaves with the character of his or her children, for there is no doubt that we as parents imprint the direction of their lives.

Shooters and hunters by definition have a deep, abiding love for the outdoors and for the traditions of hunting. For most of us, this is an important part of our lives and a reflection of who we are. The values of these pursuits, when they are done right, are those that are admired in the greater scope of society. If we are able to impart those values to our children so the values may endure, then it might be said that our lives have been successful.

There can be no argument that our future is in the children we are rearing today. If gun ownership and hunting are to survive, then it is imperative that the next generation take up the torch and continue. We hope that they too see the reasons this is important, for only then will they truly love and respect the true essence both of firearms ownership and hunting.

THE SMART APPROACH TO
STARTING KIDS HUNTING

I have always seen it as an obligation to introduce my kids to shooting and the outdoors. It's an obligation, though, that has been easy to fulfill because the need to teach them about the things that are important to me burns deep in my soul. What I have discovered along the

way is that it's a lot of fun and also that they can teach me a thing or two in the process.

If you remember nothing else, remember that kids have the attention span of a gnat. If you simply take them shooting or hunting a time or two, making sure that they are cold and bored long before you take them home, they won't say yes next time you ask. Instead, make them part of the entire process.

A YEAR-LONG, LIFE-LONG ENDEAVOR

You don't call yourself a hunter just a few weeks a year, do you? Of course not; most of us think of it as a lifestyle. We may actually hunt only a month or even a few weeks a year, but we are hunters every day of our lives. We pass the time between hunting days as we watch videos, read magazines and books, practice shooting, eat last year's venison, scout the woods and talk about hunting all year long.

So why do we exclude our kids from this and instead take them hunting a couple of times (usually on days we aren't serious about it anyway, and believe me, they can tell!) and then scratch our heads about why they aren't interested?

Make the kids part of every aspect of the hunt, but do it in small doses. Gear the approach to their ages and make it fun. There isn't an age that's too young to start. My own father had me bird hunting with him at age three. I had my children Erin and Nathan in the outdoors when they were still using bottles. Hunting depends on a love of the outdoors, so include them in every aspect. Take them fishing, camping, hiking, small-game hunting or any other outdoor activity you enjoy. It all counts.

It's a lifelong process, and as they continue to participate, it will simply

There is only one first buck in anybody's lifetime, and for a hunter it is a pivotal moment in his life. Nine-year-old Nathan Towsley took this buck with the help of his buddy Keith Mason.

be part of their lifestyle. They will likely grow up to want to come along in the years ahead, not just because it's what Dad does, but because they genuinely love hunting.

No part of the hunting process is unimportant to a child. The most mundane chore can be new and exciting to them. Use every opportunity to teach them. The key is to do it in small doses, but often. Kids can't handle lots and lots of information all at once, and they overload and grow bored. Instead, make the lessons short but frequent. A little exposure a lot of times is going to make them not only learn more, but remain interested. Make every outing a time to learn, but be

subtle about it. It shouldn't be like school; instead, it must be fun.

KEEP IT FUN

No kid, though, should be subjected to hours of the pain and endurance that sometimes is part of hunting. There is plenty of time for that later; for now, it must remain fun. To ensure that they sample those things enough to understand that it is part of hunting, but not so much as to turn them away from hunting, requires careful planning. Don't bring and I am sure others, these things are part of hunting and without some pain and suffering the hunt would somehow be diminished, it must be remembered that little kids have a much lower threshold for all this, and what may seem mild to you may be extreme to them.

Let them have a little fun. If there is not a lot of action, let them plink with their BB guns, climb a tree or just explore a little.

Make sure kids are part of the final chapter as well. Let them help with tracking and dragging the deer out of the woods. Find a job for them if you process your own deer. You might even let them pick a recipe for a venison dinner.

The saying goes that if you take your kids hunting, you won't have to be hunting for your kids. Take an interest in your kids, and not only will you teach them values that will make them grow up to be good people, but you may find that you have a built-in hunting partner for the rest of your life.

KIDS' RIFLES

The determining factor on being ready to hunt is one of maturity more than strength. Some kids are going to be ready to hunt when they are still physically small, and it's frustrating enough being a kid these days without compounding the problem by trying to learn to shoot and hunt with "adult-size" equipment.

A quick check of a dozen rifles in my gun room shows an average 13½-inch length of pull and an average overall length of about 43 inches for standard calibers, with most scoped rifles weighing at least 8 pounds, and usually more. That's a lot for those little arms to handle.

It's quite trendy right now in the gun industry to talk about taking kids hunting, and as a result, many of the gun

Kids are never too young to start being exposed to hunting and shooting. Here's a .22 rimfire in action.

your child with you when you plan to sit in a treestand for 10 hours and the temperature is 10 degrees. Leave them home if you are going to be tracking all day and plan to cover lots of miles. If the weather is extreme, bring them another time. While to me,

The best youth gun is something they can grow with. This Remington will have a longer stock installed as the young hunter grows older. The rifle is a Remington Model 700 ADL Synthetic Youth; scope is 2-7 Nikon; and ammo was Speer Nitrex 100 grain.

makers are cataloging "youth" models. Because my kids are young and new to hunting and shooting, I have been testing quite a few of these guns. In doing so, I have taken what I have come to conclude must be a unique approach.

I have had kids actually hunt with the guns!

I can, without hesitation, tell you that some of the manufacturers simply don't "get it." They cut a few inches off the barrel and the stock and call it a youth gun, but it's not even close. These guns are far too heavy for a kid to carry all day. One "youth" bolt-action rifle tips the scales at almost 8½ pounds when mounted with a small scope and equipped with a sling and five rounds of ammo. For my 10-year-old son, that's about 12 percent of his weight. An equivalent gun for me would weigh 27½ pounds. I'll be darned if I would lug a rifle that heavy! But I expect him to carry one?

The triggers are far too heavy for little hands to shoot well—often, as much as 10 percent of the kid's weight. Again, that's a 23-pound pull for me. However, if the lawyers keep designing rifles, I wouldn't be surprised to see that show up on a rifle one of these days.

With the "youth" stocks simply cut down from the adult version, often the grips are adult size and far too long a reach for little hands. It's bad enough that kids have to deal with the hard triggers, but combined with the loss of leverage resulting from the poor hand position they are forced to use, it's a wonder they can hit anything at all.

There are some exceptions, at least in the weight department. But they are almost all a result of shortening a gun that was already light and trim more than a result of any conscious design decision.

I have approached this with several manufacturers, and they all have the same response. "The market is just too small to spend any money to develop a youth gun."

My counter is, "How big is your market going to be in 10 or 20 years when the kids you fail today are doing anything but hunting?"

There are a few forward-thinking people in the gun industry who recognize that today's kids are tomorrow's future. They see that right now, the future for shooting and hunting looks tenuous at best, as fewer and fewer new hunters join our ranks.

Twelve-year-old Erin Towsley with a buck she took while hunting near Selma, Alabama. The rifle is a Remington Model 700 ADL Synthetic Youth; scope is 2-7 Nikon; and ammo was Speer Nitrex 100 grain.

The answer, of course, lies with recruiting new hunters, most of whom will come from the ranks of the youngsters in the lives of current hunters. (Also less traditional, but no less important, is a small but growing segment of new hunters who are women. They coincidentally have needs similar to young hunters when it comes to firearms design.)

The key is in searching out firearms that fit the kids but are an investment they can grow with. That means a rifle that has a full-size stock available for a later-date replacement. Your little hunting buddy will appreciate a gun that fits now and that will grow to adulthood with him or her.

KIDS & RECOIL

by a considerable margin.

Spend a little money and a lot of time at the range with young shooters before they become young hunters. Don't just hand them a big-game rifle; instead, start with a pellet or BB gun and then a .22. Finally, when they are ready, move up to a big-game gun of suitable caliber.

The .243 Win. is the minimum for deer-sized game out to 200 yards. Most new shooters will not be able to shoot well enough for hunting beyond that range, so distance is not a factor. If the game is larger, such as elk or moose, the gun must be larger as well, but the facts still apply; they just need adjustment for the situation.

When choosing a rifle for a kid or other small shooter, there are a few things to keep in mind, weight being the primary one. It's a trade-off here. A gun that's a little heavier helps reduce perceived recoil, but it can be a detriment when the hunt involves a lot of walking and the rifle must be carried all day. My experience is that most kids are recoil-sensitive, or at least think that they are. Of the two, I think they adapt to the little added weight better than they do to more recoil. Certainly, when it's time to shoot, the weight is a bonus; I can't think of a single example of when extra recoil is a good thing.

When starting a young hunter shooting with rifles appropriate for big-game hunting, the single biggest factor you will likely have to deal with is fear of recoil. It is a simple law of physics that guns powerful enough to hunt big game must kick. It cannot be avoided, so you must deal with it.

There are a few ways to reduce recoil, including muzzle brakes, good recoil pads and synthetic stocks, but nothing eliminates it completely. Anybody ready to hunt big game should be physically able to handle suitable calibers, particularly when coupled with reduction devices.

Fear of recoil is only that: fear. The best way to master it is to confront it head on, and it is only by shooting a lot and often that the fear of recoil can be mastered. Make sure that shooters have ear (and eye) protection. Not only is this mandatory shooting range safety, but noise is a big factor in shooting problems. Flinching is often as much a result of hurt ears as it is hurt shoulders. The shorter barrels used on youth guns often will increase the noise level, and any recoil-reducing muzzle brake will increase muzzle blast and noise

Proper instruction is important for safety and for learning to handle recoil.

WHAT'S AHEAD?

*I*t's evening as I write this, on the home stretch of the millennium. An hour ago, I watched the national news, and one of the big stories was about all the wildlife that's showing up in populated areas. Deer are running around inside the stores of suburban shopping malls, beavers are eating the cherry trees in Washington, D.C., coyotes are attacking kids in California and mountain lions are scaring the hell out of everybody by showing up in backyards, garages and hiking trails. We have alligators in garages and bears in backyards, and everybody's worried.

The first of the reasons given was that hunting is on the decline. Then they turned to another "expert" who went on about too many people moving into the animals' habitat and how we need to "understand the animals and get along with them in their homes." But he neglected to note that the places where the problems are happening are exactly the same places where hunting is either out of fashion or banned.

The local news, which preceded that national report, carried the latest installment in the week-long nightly saga of a black bear that's been raiding bird feeders in Vermont's most populated county. This time, the game wardens are trying to trap the bruin, and the young newscaster's talking head reported with just the right amount of gravity in her voice that they plan to kill the bear. No doubt tomorrow's newscast will show protesters demanding the bear be spared.

A few weeks ago, I had a similar

Start taking some action to defend your right to hunt, and your right to own and keep the firearms you need to do it with. Otherwise, scenes like this may only show up in the history books.

the decline because of social changes and wildlife populations getting out of hand as a result, but far too much of the human population is ignorant about nature, wildlife, guns and hunting. Yes, we are moving into the habitat of the animals, but that's been happening since this land was discovered.

The difference is that this time, the people who are intruding haven't a clue how to react to encounters with the animals. Gone is the self-reliant pioneering spirit that expanded into the wilderness and built a nation. Today, we often look to the government to solve problems—but not with the traditional management styles that have long been accepted as the solution to wildlife and man living together; this new generation of voters demands to dictate their own misguided terms.

We have become a population of "experts" who really don't know anything. With the proliferation of government by referendum, we increasingly are managing wildlife by popular opinion, and those opinions are being formed by hordes of people who never leave the hiking trails and believe all the misinformation about wildlife, hunting and firearms that they are being fed by a lying press.

It has been illustrated well with the loss of cougar and bear hunting in many places, where it has contributed to their overpopulation as well as to their loss of fear of humans. But in spite of attacks on humans—some fatal—attempts to overturn those bans have been rejected by misinformed voters. Beavers and coyotes proliferate because the price of furs dried up in response to hysterical outcries against trapping; now rabies is a big urban problem. Wildlife needs to live someplace, and if the traditional habitat is saturated by overpopulation, then they take

bear in my own backyard, tearing down and eating my neighbor's bird feeders. The difference is, I know a little about bears. I didn't call the news station or demand the game wardens come rescue us. We simply eliminated the bear's food supply, and after a couple of days, he moved on.

The problem is that not only are hunting and trapping on

what's left. If that means they must feed on groomed cherry trees, wayward poodles or the occasional child—well, they are only doing "what comes natural."

In all likelihood, this trend will only continue to escalate as our population becomes more and more urbanized and further removed from the land and nature. Hunting will see more bans, fewer new participants and a lot less public support. With more and more of the population turning against the sport, ours is a way of life that may be in its waning years.

Guns have become a four-letter word in many places, and somehow we gun owners have become responsible for many of the world's social ills. We as hunters have, for the most part, sat out that fight. Some hunters even participated in helping erode private gun ownership. After all, you don't need an "assault weapon" to hunt deer, or a handgun, a semiauto or whatever the latest buzz word happens to be. We are foolish if we ignore the patient, incremental approach of the opposition and don't realize that by the time someone comes for our bolt-action "sniper rifle," only we will be left to protest.

We may well be the last generation to enjoy hunting as we know it in America—that is, hunting that anybody can participate in. Unlike in our ancestral European homelands, the places from which many of our forefathers fled, the masses in this country can hunt. In the Old World, only the moneyed elite were privileged to hunt, and money was something you were born into. A peasant could not legally hunt and had no chance to rise above his life station.

But in America, we had a unique concept. Your pedigree mattered less than did your willingness to work and your ingenuity. For the first time in our history, wealth could be earned. Every man was free to own firearms or land, and anyone who wanted to could hunt in our great New World.

If we are not the last generation to fully benefit from that, our children may well be. Hunting is on the decline, gun ownership is under assault and private land ownership is quietly being eroded. I also believe that hunting on public, government-owned lands will also see an assault in the coming years that could perpetuate our sport's ultimate demise.

It has all happened incrementally bit by bit, and those who first raised the alarm were labeled as "extremists." By the time that they are proven right, few will be left to care.

Hunting will survive for a while, but not in the freedom-inspired, "anybody, even Joe Lunchbox, can do it" sort of way that was unique to this once wonderful country unless *we* do something, and get off our collective butts. We still

A good buck, a good rifle, a couple cartridges you're familiar with. If you care about things like these, then act now to protect wild places and your right to hunt them, as well as your constitutional right to own firearms. The future is in your hands, my hands, our hands.

may have a chance to reverse the trend, but sadly, I don't see many hunters rising to the call. Will you? Think about it.

I know I am closing this book on a somewhat pessimistic and certainly scary note, but that's our world as I see it I could say it's over let's enjoy ourselves while we can. But I can't. I won't. I love hunting, and my beautiful rifles, too much. It is up to me, and yes to *you*, to act.

GENERAL INDEX

This index outlines concepts, components, products, materials, techniques, ideas, instructions, game animals and other general references from this book. Use the Caliber Index when you're interested in locating entries for specific calibers.

CALIBER INDEX

This index lists every caliber mentioned in this book along with the page number where each reference occurs.

RIFLE NOTES

Use this space to record notes and observations regarding sight-in sessions, rifle and cartridge performance on the range and in the field, and rifle "reminders" for future shooting sessions or hunts.

RIFLE NOTES

RIFLE NOTES

RIFLE NOTES